THE ANIMAL ATLAS

Illustrated by Kenneth Lilly
Written by Barbara Taylor

BCA

LONDON · NEW YORK · SYDNEY · TORONTO

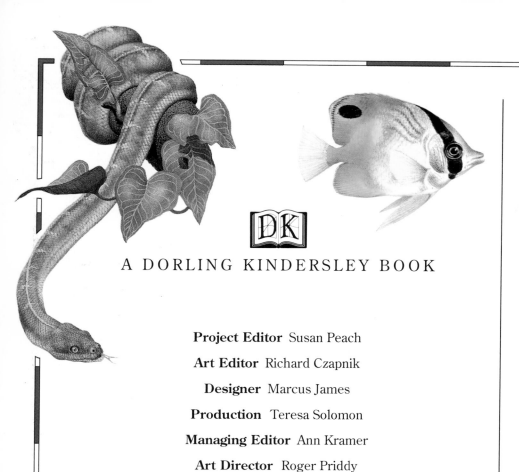

DK

A DORLING KINDERSLEY BOOK

Project Editor Susan Peach

Art Editor Richard Czapnik

Designer Marcus James

Production Teresa Solomon

Managing Editor Ann Kramer

Art Director Roger Priddy

Consultants Michael Chinery MA
and Keith Lye BA, FRGS

This edition published 1992
by BCA by arrangement with
DORLING KINDERSLEY

CN 4508

First published in Great Britain in 1992
by Dorling Kindersley Limited,
9 Henrietta Street, London WC2E 8PS

Reproduced in Singapore by Columbia Offset
Printed and bound in Italy by New Interlitho, Milan

CONTENTS

How to use this atlas

Each double-page spread in this atlas covers a particular type of habitat (the place where an animal lives). For example, the spread shown below is about European conifer forests. Habitats are arranged by continent, and there is a section in the book for each of the continents – North America, South America, Europe, Africa, Asia, Australasia, and Antarctica. The heading at the top of each page tells you which section you are in. Below you can see what the maps and symbols on each spread show, and what the abbreviations stand for.

Where on Earth?
This globe shows you where in the world the habitat featured on the spread is situated and its rough extent. On this page, for example, the red colour shows the area covered by the European conifer forests.

Latin names
Scientists have given each species of animal a Latin name, so that people all over the world can use the same name, no matter what language they speak. An animal's Latin name is divided into two parts. The first part is a group name given to a number of similar animals. For example, *Felis* is the group name given to all small cats. The second part of the name identifies the particular species of animal and often describes one of its specific characteristics. The full name for the wild cat shown here is *Felis sylvestris*, which means "cat of the woods".

Wild cat
(Felis sylvestris)

How big?
Labels next to each animal give the animal's vital statistics – its height, length, or wing-span. Like people, animals of the same species vary in size, so the measurement can only be approximate. Individual animals may be bigger or smaller than this size.

Length: 5 cm (2 in)

ABBREVIATIONS USED IN THE BOOK

mm	millimetre	sq mile	square mile
cm	centimetre	kph	kilometres per hour
in	inch	mph	miles per hour
m	metre	kg	kilogram
ft	foot	lb	pound
km	kilometre	C	centigrade
sq km	square kilometre	F	fahrenheit

Scale
You can use this scale to work out the size of the area shown on the map. The maps in the book have been drawn to different scales.

Animal symbols
The animal symbols on the map show the main area where the animals can be found, but some animals are widely distributed over the whole region. There is one symbol for each of the animals illustrated on the spread.

Map
The map shows the area of the habitat featured on the spread and surrounding regions. On these pages, for example, the map shows a large part of Europe, covering the conifer forests and the areas around them. The map also shows major geographic features in the region, and where the animals live. You can see the shape and position of the forests themselves on the globe in the top left-hand corner of the page.

Photos
The photographs around the map show you what the habitat looks like and what sort of vegetation can be found there.

Animal groups

MORE THAN A MILLION different kinds of animal have been discovered so far, but there are probably three or four times as many that people have never studied or named. Animals have several features in common.

They move, breathe, feed, grow, have young, and respond to changes in their surroundings. To make animals easier to study, biologists divide them into a number of groups. The main groups are shown below.

Invertebrates

Invertebrates (animals without backbones) were the first animals to evolve on Earth, between 600 and 1,000 million years ago. Hundreds of thousands of species are alive today, and they far outnumber the vertebrates (animals with backbones). Invertebrates come in many different shapes and sizes, including microscropic single-celled animals, corals, jellyfish, insects, snails, spiders, crabs, centipedes, and worms.

Monarch butterfly

Characteristic of invertebrates:
• do not have a backbone

The starfish is an invertebrate that lives in water. It belongs to a group called echinoderms, which means "spiky skin".

Desert tarantula

Amphibians

Amphibians evolved from fishes more than 350 million years ago. There are about 3,000 species alive today, including frogs, toads, and salamanders.

Characteristics of amphibians:
• adults live mainly on land, but breed in water
• cannot maintain a constant body temperature
• skin is usually soft with no scales
• life cycle is usually in three stages – egg, larva (or tadpole), and adult
• tadpoles breathe through gills at first, adults breathe through lungs

Japanese giant salamander

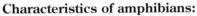
Tadpoles live in water for about 15 weeks while they develop into tiny frogs. They feed mainly on plants and small water creatures.

Green toad

Fish

Fish were the first group of vertebrates to evolve from invertebrates about 500 million years ago. There are about 22,000 species alive today – more than all the mammals, birds, reptiles, and amphibians put together. Examples include butterfly fish and sharks.

Butterfly fish

Characteristics of fish:
• adapted to live in water
• absorb oxygen from the water through gills; a few have lungs as well
• have fins to help them swim
• bodies are covered with scales

Fish have fins instead of legs. They use their fins to push and steer their way through the water.

Blue shark

Reptiles

Reptiles evolved from amphibians about 300 million years ago. About 6,100 species are alive today, including lizards, snakes, tortoises, turtles, and crocodiles. The dinosaurs were also reptiles.

Collared lizard

Characteristics of reptiles:
• cannot maintain a constant body temperature; may sleep through very hot or very cold weather
• have dry, scaly skin, sometimes with bony plates for protection
• most live and breed on land
• breathe with lungs

Turtles live in the sea but the female has to come ashore to lay her eggs, often on a sandy beach.

Western diamondback rattlesnake

Birds

Birds evolved from reptiles about 140 million years ago. There are about 9,000 species alive today, including parrots, penguins, eagles, kiwis, owls, and storks. Most birds can fly. They are adapted for flight by having wings instead of front legs, a light skeleton with hollow bones, and a covering of feathers.

Kiwi

Characteristics of birds:
• birds are the only animals with feathers
• breathe with lungs
• can maintain a constant body temperature
• lay eggs with hard, waterproof shells; usually incubate eggs with the heat of their bodies

A bird's wing is curved on top and hollowed out underneath. This shape helps the bird to glide through the air.

Scarlet macaw

Mammals

Mammals evolved from reptiles about 200 million years ago, during the age of the dinosaurs. There are more than 4,000 species alive today, including kangaroos, rats, cats, elephants, whales, bats, monkeys, and humans.

Siberian tiger

Characteristics of mammals:
• mother feeds her young on milk
• bodies are covered with fur or hair
• can maintain a constant body temperature and have sweat glands to cool their bodies
• intelligent, with large brains
• breathe with lungs

Female mammals suckle their young on milk produced in special mammary glands on their bodies.

Kangaroo rat

Animal habitats

ANIMALS LIVE ALL OVER THE WORLD, from the frozen Arctic wastes to the baking deserts. The place where an animal lives is called its habitat. Many species can live together in the same habitat because they eat different kinds of food, or make their homes in different places. The animal life in any habitat is a finely balanced mixture of species and the balance can be easily upset.

The map on these two pages shows the main types of habitat around the world. Animals have adapted to live in each of these habitats by developing characteristics which help them to survive. Similar types of habitat are found in different parts of the world and the animals that live there have developed similar adaptations. For instance, the kit fox that lives

in the North American deserts looks very like the fennec fox that lives in the Sahara Desert.

Physical barriers, such as mountains and seas, prevent many animals moving freely from one place to another. Some animals can fly or swim across these barriers, so they spread over large areas. Bats, for example, are found all over the world and tortoises can swim or float great distances across the sea, often reaching remote islands.

Deciduous woods once spread across large areas of North America and Europe, but many of them have now been cut down.

Polar and tundra
The low temperatures, biting winds, and long, dark winters make the Arctic and Antarctic very harsh environments for animals. Yet many animals do survive there, especially in the seas or on the frozen lands around the Arctic, called the tundra. In the brief summer period, many animals migrate to the Arctic to breed and raise their young.

Find out more: pages 8–9, 42–43, 59.

Coniferous forests
The largest forests in the world stretch across the top of North America, Europe, and Asia. They are called the taiga. The trees are mostly conifers, such as fir and spruce, with needle-like leaves that stay on the trees all year round. These forests provide food and shelter for many animals, especially during the cold winter months.

Find out more: pages 10–11, 28–29, 42–43.

Deciduous woodlands
Deciduous woodlands are found south of the conifer forests, where the climate is mild and and rainfall is plentiful throughout the year. The trees are mostly broadleaved species, such as oak and beech, which drop their leaves in the autumn and rest over the cooler winter months.

Find out more: pages 10–11, 30–31.

Grasslands
Grasslands grow in places where it is too dry for large areas of trees. The roots of the grasses bind the soil together and provide food for huge herds of grazing animals. There is tropical grassland, called savannah, in Africa, while the North American prairies, South American pampas and Asian steppe are examples of cooler grasslands.

Find out more: pages 10–11, 26–27, 38–39, 44–45.

Scrubland
Dusty, dry land dotted with tough shrubs and small trees is found around the Mediterranean Sea, in parts of Australia, and in California in the United States. Mos rain falls in the winter months, and animals that live in these regions have to adapt to survive the long, dry, hot summers.

Find out more:
pages 32–33.

NORTH AMERICA

The Everglades in Florida is a vast marshland area, covered with sawgrass.

Small, scrubby bushes are among the few plants that survive in the dry regions around the Mediterranean Sea.

PACIFIC OCEAN

ATLANTIC OCEAN

SOUTH AMERICA

The pampas is a huge area of grassland in South America. Much of it is used by farmers for grazing cattle.

A N T A R

Deserts

It hardly ever rains in the deserts, so the animals that live there have to survive without drinking for long periods or get all the water they need from their food. They also have to cope with boiling hot days and freezing cold nights. Many animals come out only at dawn and dusk when it is cooler and more humid.

Find out more: pages 14–15, 34–35, 44–45, 52–53.

Rainforests

Rainforests grow near the Equator, where the weather is warm and humid all year round. Most of the trees are evergreen with broad leaves. Rainforests contain the richest variety of wildlife to be found anywhere on Earth. More than 50 per cent of all the different kinds of plants and animals in the world live in the rainforests.

Find out more: pages 24–25, 36–37, 54–55.

Marshland and swamp

Marshy, waterlogged places develop near lakes and rivers and along coasts. One of the largest marshland areas is the Everglades in Florida. Mangrove swamps often fringe the coasts in tropical areas. Both these habitats are rich in food supplies and places to breed, and provide homes for a wide variety of animals, especially birds and insects.

Find out more: pages 16–17

Mountains

Mountains are found in both warm and cold regions of the world. They provide a wide range of habitats for wildlife, from forests on the lower slopes to grassland and tundra farther up. The higher up you go, the colder it becomes. Above a certain height – called the tree line – the temperature is too low for trees to survive. Even higher up is the snow line. Above this it is so cold that the ground is always covered in snow and ice. The climate in mountainous regions can be severe, with low temperatures, fierce winds, and low rainfall. Mountain animals also have to cope with steep, slippery slopes.

Find out more: pages 12–13, 22–23, 46–47.

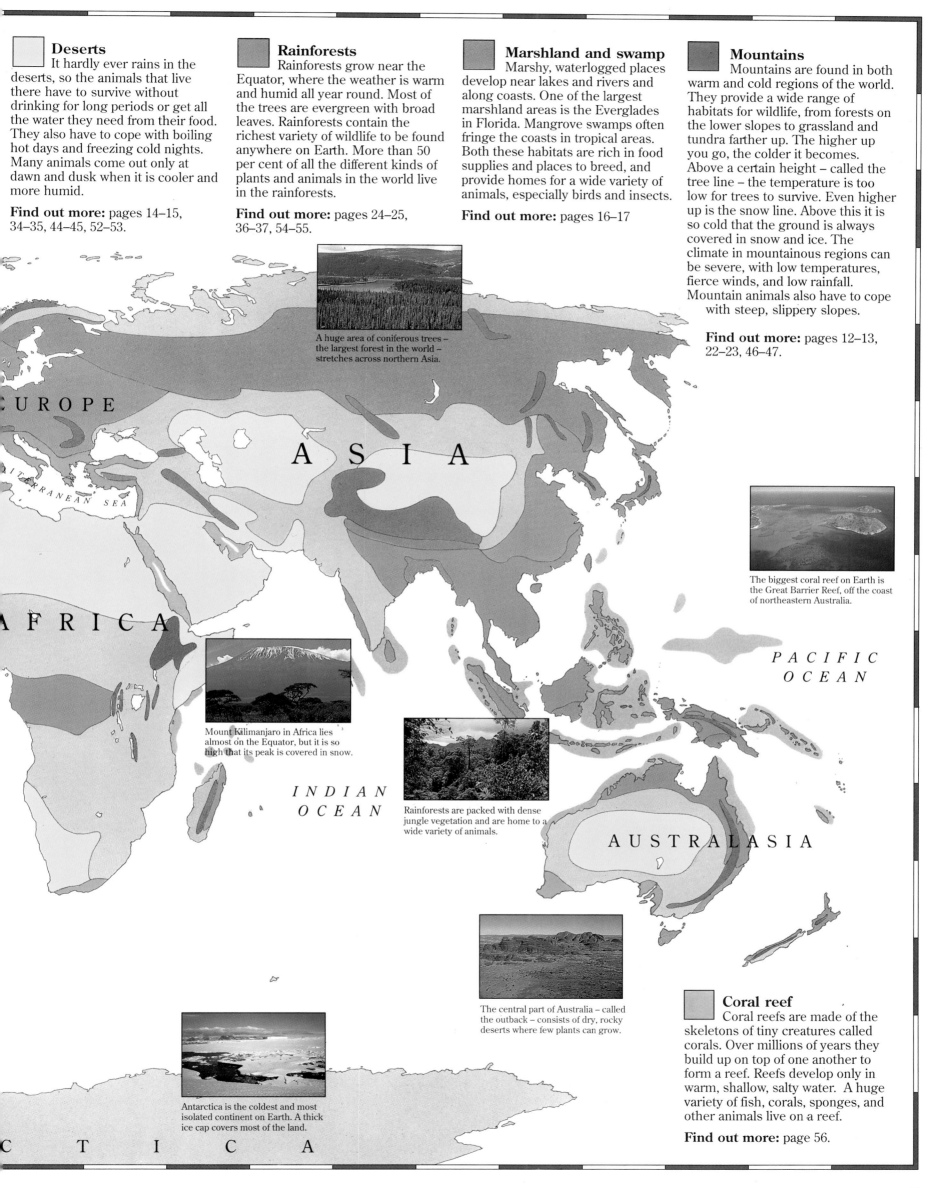

A huge area of coniferous trees – the largest forest in the world – stretches across northern Asia.

EUROPE

MEDITERRANEAN SEA

ASIA

AFRICA

The biggest coral reef on Earth is the Great Barrier Reef, off the coast of northeastern Australia.

PACIFIC OCEAN

Mount Kilimanjaro in Africa lies almost on the Equator, but it is so high that its peak is covered in snow.

INDIAN OCEAN

Rainforests are packed with dense jungle vegetation and are home to a wide variety of animals.

AUSTRALASIA

The central part of Australia – called the outback – consists of dry, rocky deserts where few plants can grow.

Antarctica is the coldest and most isolated continent on Earth. A thick ice cap covers most of the land.

ANTARCTICA

Coral reef

Coral reefs are made of the skeletons of tiny creatures called corals. Over millions of years they build up on top of one another to form a reef. Reefs develop only in warm, shallow, salty water. A huge variety of fish, corals, sponges, and other animals live on a reef.

Find out more: page 56.

The Arctic

THE ARCTIC consists of the northernmost parts of North America, Europe, and Asia, and a huge area of frozen ocean around the North Pole. It is one of the coldest places on Earth. The temperature rarely rises above 10°C (50°F), and in the winter it often drops to -40°C (-40°F). During the brief summer period, it is light for 24 hours a day. Light and warmth encourage the growth of tiny sea animals and plants called plankton, which are eaten by fishes, seals, and birds. On land, flowers bloom, providing food for millions of insects. Many birds, such as the Arctic tern and the brent goose, take advantage of this insect food supply by migrating to the Arctic to breed and raise their young. When the winter sets in again, these birds return to warmer climates. Some seals and whales also migrate south to find warmer water.

Food store
During the summer the Arctic fox stores food, such as dead birds and eggs, underneath rocks. Thanks to the cold climate, this food keeps as well as it would in a refrigerator. The fox eats it in the winter months, when fresh food is hard to find. The Arctic fox has a thick fur coat, and can survive in temperatures as low as -50°C (-58°F).

Arctic fox
(*Alopex lagopus*)
Body length: up to 70 cm (2 ft 3 in)
Tail: up to 40 cm (16 in)

Bearded seal
(*Erignathus barbatus*)
Length: up to 2.5 m (8 ft 2 in)

Wonderful whiskers
The bearded seal lives in the seas around the edge of the ice cap. It has long, sensitive whiskers which it uses to feel for shellfish on the sea bed. It also feeds on fish and prawns. In spring, the female hauls herself on to the ice to give birth.

Reindeer warble-fly
(*Oedemagena tarandi*)
Length: 1.5 cm (0.5 in)

Hooded seal
(*Cystophora cristata*)
Length: up to 3 m (9 ft 9 in)

Fearsome fly
The reindeer warble-fly lays its eggs in the fur of caribou and reindeer, which migrate to the Arctic in summer. When the eggs hatch, the grubs burrow through the skin and live in the deer's flesh. Eventually, the grubs fall to the ground where they develop into adults.

Balloon nose
The male hooded seal has a strange balloon-like structure on the end of his nose. In the breeding season, he blows air into this structure, which can become 30 cm (12 in) long. The air in the "balloon" amplifies the loud calls which he makes to warn off other males. The hooded seal spends most of its life at sea, searching for fish and squid. It only comes out on to the ice to mate, breed, and moult.

Musk ox
(*Ovibos moschatus*)
Height at shoulder: up to 1.5 m (5 ft)
Horns: up to 70 cm (2 ft 3 in)

Lethal paws
The polar bear is a huge animal and can weigh as much as 10 adult people. It feeds mainly on seals, and often catches them at holes in the ice when they come up for air. One swipe from the bear's massive paws is enough to kill a seal. The bear then uses its claws to grab and hold on to its prey.

Polar bear
(*Thalarctos maritimus*)
Height at shoulder: up to 1.6 m (5 ft 3 in)
Body length: up to 2.5 m (8 ft 2 in)

Longest hair
The musk ox has the longest coat of any mammal. Some hairs in its outer coat are nearly 1 m (3 ft 3 in) in length. If a group of musk oxen are attacked, they form a tight circle and defend themselves with their sharp horns. The young stand in the middle of the circle for protection.

Narwhal
(*Monodon monoceros*)
Body length: up to 4.6 m (15 ft)
Tusk: 3 m (9 ft 10 in)

Arctic unicorn
The narwhal is a mammal, related to whales and dolphins. It has only two teeth. One of the male's teeth grows into a long, spiralling tusk, which sticks out through a hole in his top lip. No-one knows what this tusk is for, although males have been seen fighting one another with their tusks.

Champion migrator
The Arctic tern raises its chicks in the Arctic during the brief summer period. Then it flies 13,000 km (8,000 miles) to Antarctica, to take advantage of the summer months there when plenty of food is available. This is the longest migration route of any bird. An Arctic tern can live for 30 years or more, so it may travel more than 800,000 km (500,000 miles) in its lifetime.

Sea canary
Beluga or white whales communicate with each other using a variety of songs. Nineteenth century sailors used to call them "sea canaries" because of all the sounds they make. They also make clicking noises which bounce off objects around them and help them to find their way around. In winter, beluga whales gather together in huge herds and migrate south.

Arctic tern
(*Sterna paradisaea*)
Length: 35 cm (14 in)

Beluga whale
(*Delphinapterus leucas*)
Length: up to 6.1 m (20 ft)

Arctic hare (*Lepus arcticus*)
Body length: up to 60 cm (2 ft)
Tail: up to 8 cm (3 in)

NORTH AMERICA

MUSK OX

BEAUFORT SEA

REINDEER WARBLE-FLY

BANKS ISLAND

EIDER DUCK

BELUGA WHALE

ARCTIC CIRCLE

ASIA

Lena

Oleněk

POLAR BEAR

LAPTEV SEA

Few animals live on the frozen polar ice cap, as there are no plants or insects to provide food.

ARCTIC TERN

ARCTIC FOX

ELLESMERE ISLAND

BAFFIN ISLAND

A R C T I C

• NORTH POLE

O C E A N

BEARDED SEAL

ARCTIC HARE

NARWHAL

WALRUS

Areas of the Arctic that are not permanently covered in ice are known as tundra.

G R E E N L A N D

HOODED SEAL

Much of the island of Greenland is covered in flowing rivers of ice, called glaciers.

Changing colour
The Arctic hare can change the colour of its coat to match its surroundings. In the winter, its fur is white. This makes it hard to see against the snow. In summer, when the snow melts, the hare sheds its white fur and grows a grey-brown coat. In the far north of the Arctic, where there is always snow, these hares stay white all year round.

A T L A N T I C
O C E A N

ICELAND

N O R W E G I A N
S E A

KILOMETRES
0   300   600   900

MILES
0   300   600

Eider duck
(*Somateria mollisima*)
Length: up to 60 cm (2 ft)

Island nests
The eider duck breeds among clumps of grass on small islands in the Arctic Ocean. These remote nesting sites help to protect the young from enemies. The female bird plucks soft down feathers from her breast and uses them to line the nest. If the parent birds have to leave the nest, they pull the down over the eggs. This keeps the eggs warm and helps to hide them from enemies, such as gulls and foxes.

Walrus
(*Odobenus rosmarus*)
Length: up to 3.5 m (11 ft 5 in)
Tusks: up to 90 cm (35 in)

Digging teeth
The walrus has long tusks which it uses to dig up shellfish and other small animals from the sea bed. Walruses live in large groups and spend much of the day sleeping on the ice. In the breeding season, walruses gather together in traditional areas and males compete against each other to win mates.

Forests, Lakes, and Prairies

THE EVERGREEN FORESTS OF CANADA consist of dense areas of spruce, pine, and fir trees. These forests are marshy underfoot and contain many lakes. Farther south, forests of oak, hickory, and chestnut trees once spread right across the eastern part of North America. Today, vast areas of these forests have been destroyed for timber or to clear land for farming. Some of the forest animals, such as the raccoon and the opossum, have adapted to this new environment, but many animals have declined in numbers, or retreated to the hills and mountains.

The prairies once formed a huge sea of grass. Millions of bison and pronghorn antelope used to graze on the prairies, but they were almost wiped out by hunters during the 19th century. Both animals are now protected species. Today much of this region is used for farming.

Sage grouse
(*Centrocercus urophasianus*)
Length: up to 46 cm (18 in)

Big cheeks

The least chipmunk has large cheek pouches which it uses to carry food back to its underground burrow. Inside the burrow are several chambers used for storing food, and living and nesting chambers. In winter, the chipmunk hibernates in the burrow.

Raccoon
(*Procyon lotor*)
Body length:
up to 66 cm (2 ft 2 in)
Tail: up to 30 cm (12 in)

Dustbin raider

The raccoon has long, sensitive fingers which it uses to search for food. It often comes into cities and raids dustbins for leftover food scraps. The raccoon's thick fur coat keeps it warm during the cold winter months.

Flavoured flesh

The sage grouse feeds on the leaves of the sagebrush plant. Eventually its flesh takes on a strong sage flavour. During the spring, the male puts on a special display to win a mate. He puffs out his chest feathers, opens and closes his tail, and inflates the air sacs on his neck. He also makes loud, booming calls.

Two-spotted ladybird
(*Adalia bipunctata*)
Length: 5 mm (0.25 in)

Pest control

The two-spotted ladybird is common throughout North America and is found in a range of habitats, including forests, fields, and gardens. It feeds on small insects and helps to keep down the number of pests in gardens and fields. The ladybird's hard, red wing cases protect its soft wings and body underneath.

Least chipmunk
(*Eutamias minimus*)
Body length: up to 11 cm (4.5 in)
Tail: up to 11 cm (4.5 in)

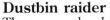

YUKON **BALD EAGLE**   **MOOSE**

The forest lakes are home to many water birds, including gulls, ducks, and swans.

Bugle bird

The whooping crane is named after its bugle-like, whooping call. It nests only in a remote area of northwest Canada. By the 1940s the whooping crane had been almost wiped out by hunting. It is now a protected species.

Moose (*Alces alces*)
Height at shoulder:
up to 2 m (6 ft 6 in)
Length: up to 3 m (10 ft)

Heavyweight deer

The moose is the largest deer in the world. In the autumn, a male may weigh more than 450 kg (1,000 lbs). The moose has broad hooves and long legs, which help it to travel through deep snow, bogs, or lakes. Its overhanging top lip enables the moose to tear off leaves and branches. In the autumn, the male uses his antlers to fight other males and win mates.

Whooping crane
(*Grus americana*)
Height: 1.5 m (5 ft)
Wingspan: 2.2 m (7 ft 6 in)

Today the flat plains of the prairies are used for growing wheat.

Barking burrower

The prairie dog is a type of squirrel that lives in networks of tunnels under the prairies. Its name comes from the barking noise it makes when it is alarmed. Before people started to farm the region, prairie dog colonies used to cover vast areas and contained millions of inhabitants.

Prairie dog (*Cynomys ludovicianus*)
Body length: up to 35 cm (14 in)
Tail: 8 cm (3 in)

White head

The bald eagle – the symbol of the United States – gets its name from its white head. An old meaning of the word "bald" is "white". In a spectacular courtship display, the male and the female bird lock talons in flight and somersault through the air. The pair build a huge nest of sticks, weeds, and soil and add to it each year.

Bald eagle
(*Haliaeetus leucocephalus*)
Length: 81 cm (2 ft 8 in)
Wingspan: up to
2.2 m (7 ft 6 in)

Monarch butterfly
(*Danaus plexippus*)
Wingspan: up to
10 cm (4 in)

Dam builder

The beaver has powerful jaws and strong front teeth. It gnaws through tree trunks and uses them to build a dam across a river. In the pond that forms behind the dam, the beaver builds a lodge of sticks and mud, where it hibernates.

Terrific traveller

In autumn, the monarch butterfly migrates from Canada to California, Mexico, or the Caribbean – a journey of more than 3,200 km (2,000 miles). It travels north again in the spring, but stops on the way to mate and then die. Its offspring complete the journey north.

Wolverine (*Gulo gulo*)
Height at shoulder: 38 cm (15 in)
Body length: up to 86 cm (2 ft 10 in)

Crushing bite

The fierce wolverine is strong for its size and has a powerful, crushing bite. It has been known to kill animals as large as a caribou. The wolverine's widespread toes help it to bound across snow as it chases its prey. A wolverine can travel over 65 km (40 miles) without resting.

Beaver
(*Castor canadensis*)
Body length: up to 96 cm (3 ft 2 in)
Tail: up to 30 cm (12 in)

Blue jay
(*Cyanocitta cristata*)
Length: 25 cm (10 in)

Aerial view of autumn trees in the deciduous forests of New England.

Tree planter

The blue jay often buries acorns and other tree seeds to eat later. Some of these seeds survive to grow into new trees, helping the forest to spread. In spring and autumn, large flocks of blue jays migrate south to warmer climates.

Great Bear Lake

WOLVERINE

WHOOPING CRANE

Great Slave Lake

TWO-SPOTTED LADYBIRD

Mackenzie

Peace

N O R T H

RACCOON

BLUE JAY

Lake Winnipeg

MONARCH BUTTERFLY

LEAST CHIMPMUNK

H U D S O N
B A Y

St Lawrence

M E R I C A

Missouri

SAGE GROUSE

GREAT LAKES

BEAVER

Great Salt Lake

PRAIRIE DOG

OPOSSUM

Colorado

Arkansas

Red

Mississippi

APPALACHIAN MTS

ATLANTIC OCEAN

Rio Grande

KILOMETRES
0   400   800   1200

0   400   800
MILES

Opossum (*Didelphis virginiana*)
Body length: up to 53 cm (21 in)
Tail: up to 50 cm (20 in)

Baby pouch

The opossum is North America's only pouched mammal. The young climb into the mother's pouch after birth and stay there for several months, feeding on her milk. To escape an enemy, the opossum sometimes "plays dead", and may stay in a trance-like state for several hours.

The Rockies

THE ROCKIES ARE A VAST range of mountains that stretch down the western side of North America. The Rockies form a barrier to the moist winds which sweep towards the continent from the Pacific Ocean. As these winds rise up over the mountains and cool, the water they carry falls as rain or snow. On the mountain peaks, winds can reach 320 kph (200 mph) and temperatures may fall to -51°C (-60°F).

The Rockies provide a refuge for animals that have been hunted or driven out of other habitats by people. Some species are specially adapted for climbing and jumping on the mountain slopes. Many of the animals have warm fur to protect them against the cold and the winds. In winter, some of them shelter in the forests on the lower slopes.

Phoebus butterfly
(*Parnassius phoebus*)
Wingspan: up to
9 cm (3.5 in)

Summer butterfly
Male phoebus butterflies appear in the Rockies in mid-summer, eight to ten days before the females. They mate soon after the female hatches from the pupa – often even before she is able to fly.

Spiky armour
The porcupine's furry coat hides about 30,000 spiky hairs, called quills. If it is threatened, the porcupine turns its back, raises its quills and lashes its tail. Its tail quills are barbed like arrows, so that they stick into an enemy's skin.

Porcupine
(*Erethizon dorsatum*)
Body length: up to
76 cm (2 ft 6 in)
Tail: up to 28 cm (11 in)

Grizzled giant
The huge grizzly bear gets its name from the whitish (grizzled) tips to its hairs. A grizzly can kill an animal as large as a moose or caribou, but it usually feeds on smaller animals, fish, and plants. It has long front claws which it uses to kill prey. A grizzly can run as fast as a horse for short distances and may stand up on its back legs to get a better view of its prey. In autumn, the grizzly eats as much as possible to build up stores of fat to last it through its winter hibernation.

Grizzly bear
(*Ursus arctos horribilis*)
Height standing on back
legs: up to 3 m (10 ft)

Non-skid feet
The bighorn sheep is good at climbing and jumping on the steep mountain slopes. Each of its hooves is divided into two halves which separate to help the sheep grip the rocks. The male has curving horns, which he uses to fight rival males in the breeding season.

Bighorn sheep (*Ovis canadensis*)
Body length: up to 1.8 m (6 ft)
Horns: up to 90 cm (3 ft)

Winter white
In summer the snowshoe hare has brown fur, but in winter it grows a white coat which camouflages it against the snow. It also develops dense fur on its feet, making them look like snowshoes. The fur keeps the hare's feet warm and stops it sinking into the snow.

Snowshoe hare
(*Lepus americanus*)
Length: up to 50 cm (20 in)

Spotted camouflage
The bobcat's spotted coat helps it to blend in with a rocky or forested background, so that it can creep up on its prey without being seen. The bobcat usually feeds on rabbits and hares, but will eat almost any reptile, mammal, or bird. It can even kill a deer, which provides enough food for a week or more.

Bobcat
(*Lynx rufus*)
Height at shoulder:
25 cm (10 in)
Length: up to
1 m (3 ft 3 in)

Tree glider

The northern flying squirrel glides from tree to tree using flaps of skin along the sides of its body which unfold like wings. The squirrel controls its glide by moving its legs and using its tail as a rudder to change direction. It can glide up to 38 m (125 ft).

Northern flying squirrel
(*Glaucomys sabrinus*)
Body length: up to 15 cm (6 in)
Tail: up to 13 cm (5 in)

Rocky mountain goat
(*Oreamnos americanus*)
Height to shoulder: up to 1 m (3 ft 3 in)

Clinging toes

The Rocky Mountain goat has curved toes. They help it to cling to steep slopes and rocky crags where it is safe from most enemies. Baby goats can stand up minutes after they are born, and are able to follow their mother over the steep slopes within days.

Insect catcher

The mountain bluebird eats seeds, berries, and insects. It darts out from a perch to snatch any insects flying past or flies low and pounces on its prey on the ground.

Ptarmigan
(*Lagopus leucurus*)
Length: 33 cm (13 in)

Mountain bluebird
(*Sialia currucoides*)
Length: up to 19 cm (7.5 in)

Prowling pouncer

The mountain lion (also called the puma or cougar) stalks its prey at night. It creeps up on its victim and then pounces on it from an overhanging tree or rock. Long, sharp claws help the mountain lion to hold its prey, which it kills by biting through the neck.

ARCTIC OCEAN

Feathered feet

The ptarmigan's feathered feet help it to keep warm and stop it sinking into the snow. During the breeding season in spring and summer, the female's striped feathers camouflage her on the nest. In winter both the male and female grow white feathers to hide them on the snow.

Mountain lion (*Felis concolor*)
Height at shoulder: 63 cm (2 ft 1 in)
Body length: up to 1.5 m (5 ft)

Many of North America's great rivers, such as the Missouri, start in the Rockies.

Up to 60 m (200 ft) of snow may fall on the Rockies each year.

The slopes of the Rockies are covered by fir and pine trees.

Wapiti
(*Cervus elaphus*)
Height at shoulder:
1.6 m (5 ft 6 in)
Antlers: up to 1.5 m (5 ft)

Amazing antlers

The wapiti is a type of deer. During the autumn breeding season, the males fight one another with their huge antlers to win mates. A male's antlers can weigh up to 11 kg (25 lbs). The name wapiti comes from the American Indian word for "white", and refers to the white patch on the animal's rear.

Yukon

GULF OF ALASKA

GRIZZLY BEAR

PTARMIGAN

SNOWSHOE HARE

NORTHERN FLYING SQUIRREL

ROCKY MOUNTAIN GOAT

BIGHORN SHEEP

Great Bear Lake

Great Slave Lake

PACIFIC OCEAN

WAPITI

PORCUPINE

Lake Winnipeg

N O R T H

A M E R I C A

PHOEBUS BUTTERFLY

BOBCAT

GREAT PLAINS

COAST RANGES

SIERRA NEVADA

MOUNTAIN BLUEBIRD

Great Salt Lake

Colorado

Missouri

MOUNTAIN LION

KILOMETRES
0   250   500   750

0   250   500
MILES

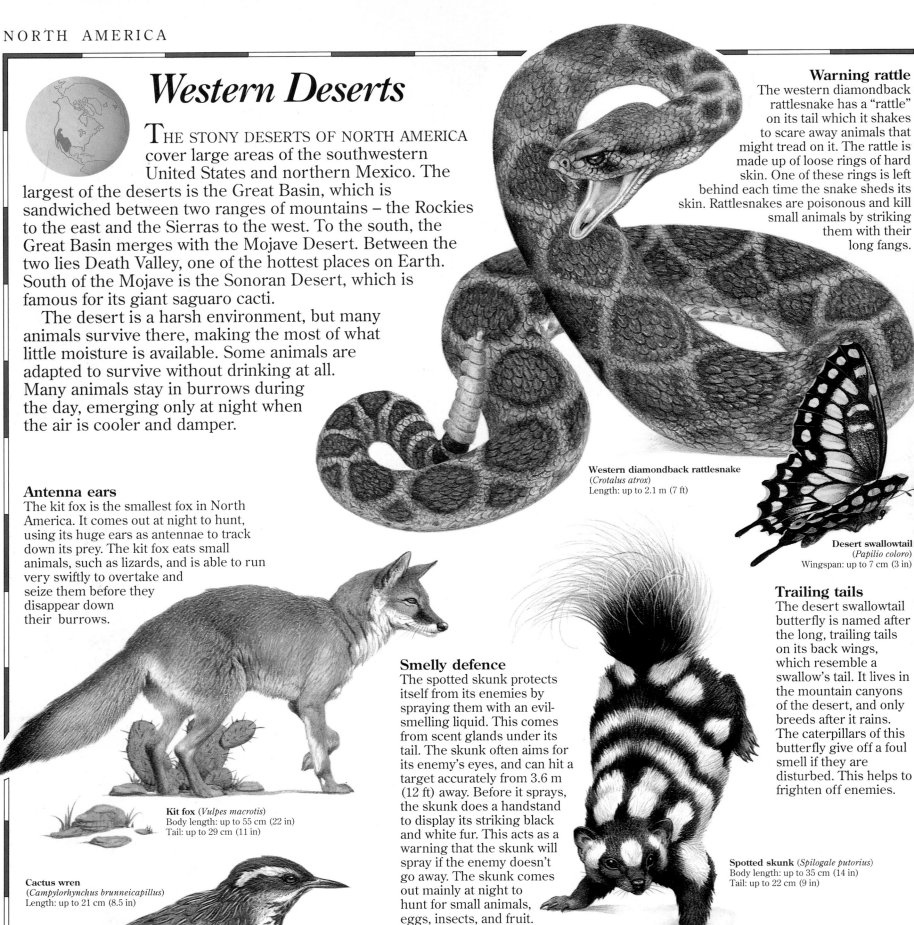

Western Deserts

THE STONY DESERTS OF NORTH AMERICA cover large areas of the southwestern United States and northern Mexico. The largest of the deserts is the Great Basin, which is sandwiched between two ranges of mountains – the Rockies to the east and the Sierras to the west. To the south, the Great Basin merges with the Mojave Desert. Between the two lies Death Valley, one of the hottest places on Earth. South of the Mojave is the Sonoran Desert, which is famous for its giant saguaro cacti.

The desert is a harsh environment, but many animals survive there, making the most of what little moisture is available. Some animals are adapted to survive without drinking at all. Many animals stay in burrows during the day, emerging only at night when the air is cooler and damper.

Warning rattle
The western diamondback rattlesnake has a "rattle" on its tail which it shakes to scare away animals that might tread on it. The rattle is made up of loose rings of hard skin. One of these rings is left behind each time the snake sheds its skin. Rattlesnakes are poisonous and kill small animals by striking them with their long fangs.

Western diamondback rattlesnake
(*Crotalus atrox*)
Length: up to 2.1 m (7 ft)

Desert swallowtail
(*Papilio coloro*)
Wingspan: up to 7 cm (3 in)

Antenna ears
The kit fox is the smallest fox in North America. It comes out at night to hunt, using its huge ears as antennae to track down its prey. The kit fox eats small animals, such as lizards, and is able to run very swiftly to overtake and seize them before they disappear down their burrows.

Kit fox (*Vulpes macrotis*)
Body length: up to 55 cm (22 in)
Tail: up to 29 cm (11 in)

Smelly defence
The spotted skunk protects itself from its enemies by spraying them with an evil-smelling liquid. This comes from scent glands under its tail. The skunk often aims for its enemy's eyes, and can hit a target accurately from 3.6 m (12 ft) away. Before it sprays, the skunk does a handstand to display its striking black and white fur. This acts as a warning that the skunk will spray if the enemy doesn't go away. The skunk comes out mainly at night to hunt for small animals, eggs, insects, and fruit.

Trailing tails
The desert swallowtail butterfly is named after the long, trailing tails on its back wings, which resemble a swallow's tail. It lives in the mountain canyons of the desert, and only breeds after it rains. The caterpillars of this butterfly give off a foul smell if they are disturbed. This helps to frighten off enemies.

Spotted skunk (*Spilogale putorius*)
Body length: up to 35 cm (14 in)
Tail: up to 22 cm (9 in)

Cactus wren
(*Campylorhynchus brunneicapillus*)
Length: up to 21 cm (8.5 in)

Spiny fortress
The cactus wren builds a large, domed nest among the spines of a cactus or a thorny bush, where its young are well protected from enemies. The bird's tough feathers and hard, scaly legs protect it from scratches. The wren may also build several extra nests, where it roosts during the winter.

Roadrunner
(*Geococcyx californianus*)
Body length: up to 60 cm (2 ft)
Tail: 30 cm (12 in)

Speedy bird
The roadrunner lives on the ground and rarely flies. It has extremely powerful legs and can run at speeds of up to 24 kph (15 mph). Its long tail acts as a brake or rudder, allowing the bird to swerve suddenly or come to an abrupt halt. The roadrunner is very strong, and can kill a snake with one bite from its sharp beak.

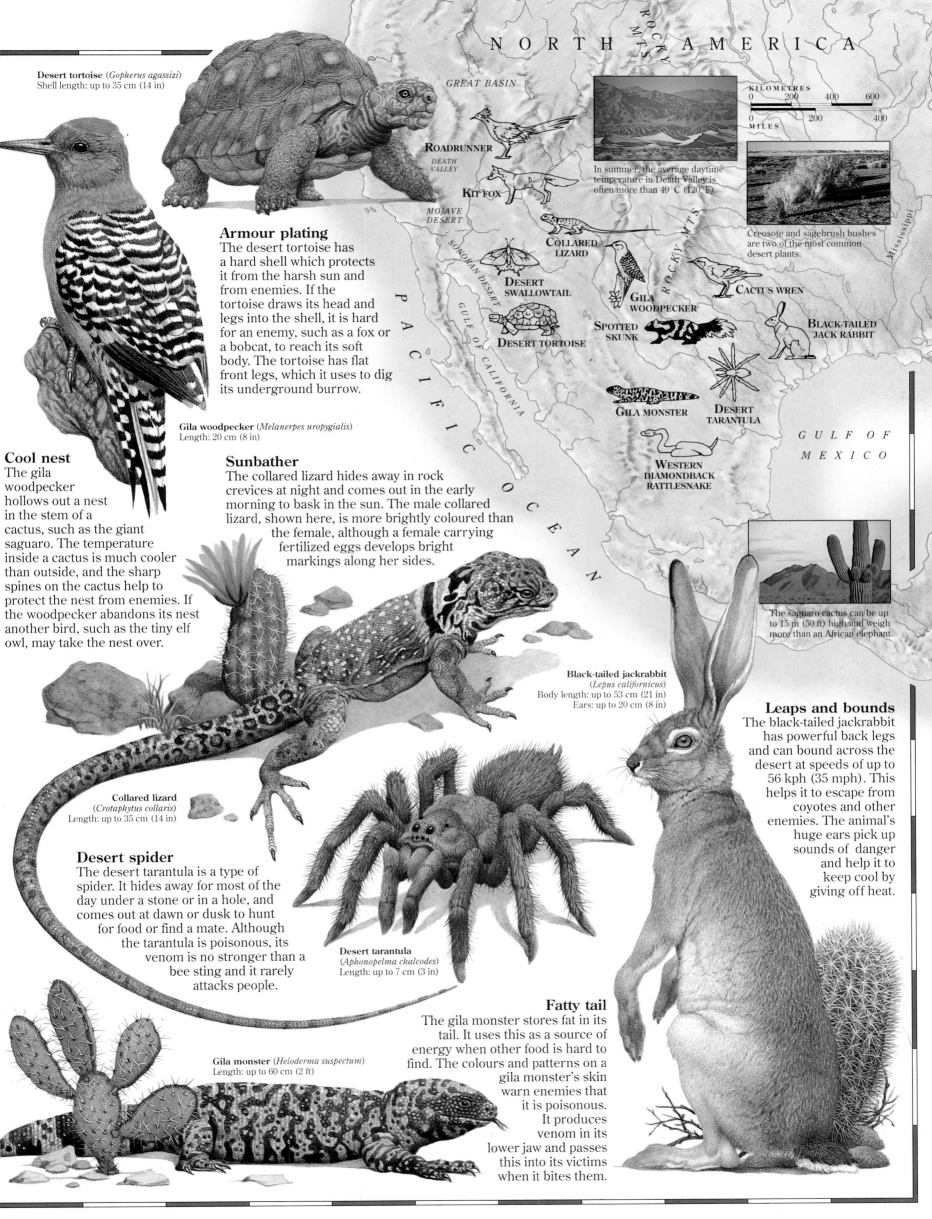

Desert tortoise (*Gopherus agassizi*)
Shell length: up to 35 cm (14 in)

GREAT BASIN

ROCKY MTS

ROADRUNNER

DEATH VALLEY

KIT FOX

MOJAVE DESERT

COLLARED LIZARD

SONORAN DESERT

DESERT SWALLOWTAIL

GILA WOODPECKER

CACTUS WREN

SPOTTED SKUNK

BLACK-TAILED JACK RABBIT

DESERT TORTOISE

GILA MONSTER

DESERT TARANTULA

ROCKY MTS

P A C I F I C   O C E A N

GULF OF CALIFORNIA

WESTERN DIAMONDBACK RATTLESNAKE

GULF OF MEXICO

Mississippi

KILOMETRES
0   200   400   600
MILES
0   200   400

In summer, the average daytime temperature in Death Valley is often more than 49°C (120°F).

Creosote and sagebrush bushes are two of the most common desert plants.

The saguaro cactus can be up to 15 m (50 ft) high and weigh more than an African elephant.

Armour plating
The desert tortoise has a hard shell which protects it from the harsh sun and from enemies. If the tortoise draws its head and legs into the shell, it is hard for an enemy, such as a fox or a bobcat, to reach its soft body. The tortoise has flat front legs, which it uses to dig its underground burrow.

Gila woodpecker (*Melanerpes uropygialis*)
Length: 20 cm (8 in)

Cool nest
The gila woodpecker hollows out a nest in the stem of a cactus, such as the giant saguaro. The temperature inside a cactus is much cooler than outside, and the sharp spines on the cactus help to protect the nest from enemies. If the woodpecker abandons its nest another bird, such as the tiny elf owl, may take the nest over.

Sunbather
The collared lizard hides away in rock crevices at night and comes out in the early morning to bask in the sun. The male collared lizard, shown here, is more brightly coloured than the female, although a female carrying fertilized eggs develops bright markings along her sides.

Collared lizard
(*Crotaphytus collaris*)
Length: up to 35 cm (14 in)

Desert spider
The desert tarantula is a type of spider. It hides away for most of the day under a stone or in a hole, and comes out at dawn or dusk to hunt for food or find a mate. Although the tarantula is poisonous, its venom is no stronger than a bee sting and it rarely attacks people.

Desert tarantula
(*Aphonopelma chalcodes*)
Length: up to 7 cm (3 in)

Black-tailed jackrabbit
(*Lepus californicus*)
Body length: up to 53 cm (21 in)
Ears: up to 20 cm (8 in)

Leaps and bounds
The black-tailed jackrabbit has powerful back legs and can bound across the desert at speeds of up to 56 kph (35 mph). This helps it to escape from coyotes and other enemies. The animal's huge ears pick up sounds of danger and help it to keep cool by giving off heat.

Fatty tail
The gila monster stores fat in its tail. It uses this as a source of energy when other food is hard to find. The colours and patterns on a gila monster's skin warn enemies that it is poisonous. It produces venom in its lower jaw and passes this into its victims when it bites them.

Gila monster (*Heloderma suspectum*)
Length: up to 60 cm (2 ft)

The Everglades

THE SEMI-TROPICAL MARSHLAND of the Everglades National Park covers an area of 5,490 sq km (2,120 sq miles) in southern Florida in the United States. The Everglades is an enormous swamp, with deeper channels of water running through it. Grass covers most of the swamp, broken only by islands of trees. There are two main seasons in the Everglades: the wet summer and the dry winter. In the summer, the higher water levels allow the animals to move freely throughout the park. But in winter they gather around the few remaining water holes.

The park provides a rich feeding and breeding ground for large numbers of insects, fish, reptiles, and birds. Many rare animals, such as the Florida panther and the manatee, live there. Unfortunately, the Everglades is threatened by drainage schemes to the north of the park and by pesticides and fertilizers used on neighbouring farms, which are polluting the water.

Loggerhead turtle
(*Caretta caretta*)
Length: up to 1.2 m (4 ft)

Dangerous journey
The female loggerhead turtle comes ashore at night to lay her eggs on the beach. She digs a hole, lays more than a hundred eggs, covers them with sand and then heads back to sea. After about eight weeks, the baby turtles hatch out and make their way as quickly as they can to the safety of the sea. Many of them are eaten by sea birds, such as gulls and skuas, before they can get there.

American alligator
(*Alligator mississippiensis*)
Length: up to 3.6m (12 ft)

Poisonous butterfly
The caterpillar of the zebra butterfly feeds on passion flower vines, which are poisonous to most animals. The poison stays in its body, even when it becomes an adult butterfly, and protects it from its enemies.

Zebra butterfly (*Heliconius charitonius*)
Wingspan: up to 8.5 cm (3 in)

Everglade kite (*Rostrhamus sociabilis*)
Length: up to 46 cm (18 in)
Wingspan: 1.1 m (3 ft 8 in)

Hole maker
American alligators clean out large holes in the floor of the swamp. During the dry season, when the Everglades dries up, these holes stay filled with water. Turtles, garfish, and other animals often take refuge there, and provide the alligators with food.

Islands of trees, called hammocks, stick up above the water level.

Snail diet
The Everglade kite is also called the "snail kite" because it eats only one type of water snail, called *Pomacea*. The kite uses its slender, hooked beak to prise out the snail's soft body without breaking its shell. Everglade kites nest in huge colonies and search for food in groups.

Heat sensors
The cottonmouth snake hunts at night. Like all members of the pit viper family, it has two small holes, called pits, on its face. These pits sense heat and help the snake to find the warm bodies of small animals and birds in the dark. The cottonmouth kills its prey with its poisonous fangs.

Super diver
The brown pelican feeds on fish. It catches its prey by making a spectacular dive into the sea and scooping up a mouthful of fishes and water in the huge pouch under its beak. Often this water weighs twice as much as the bird itself. A brown pelican can scoop up a fish in less than two seconds.

Brown pelican (*Pelecanus occidentalis*)
Length: up to 1.3 m (4 ft 6 in)
Wingspan: 2.5 m (8 ft 2 in)

Cottonmouth (*Agkistrodon piscivorus*)
Length: up to 1.8 m (6 ft)

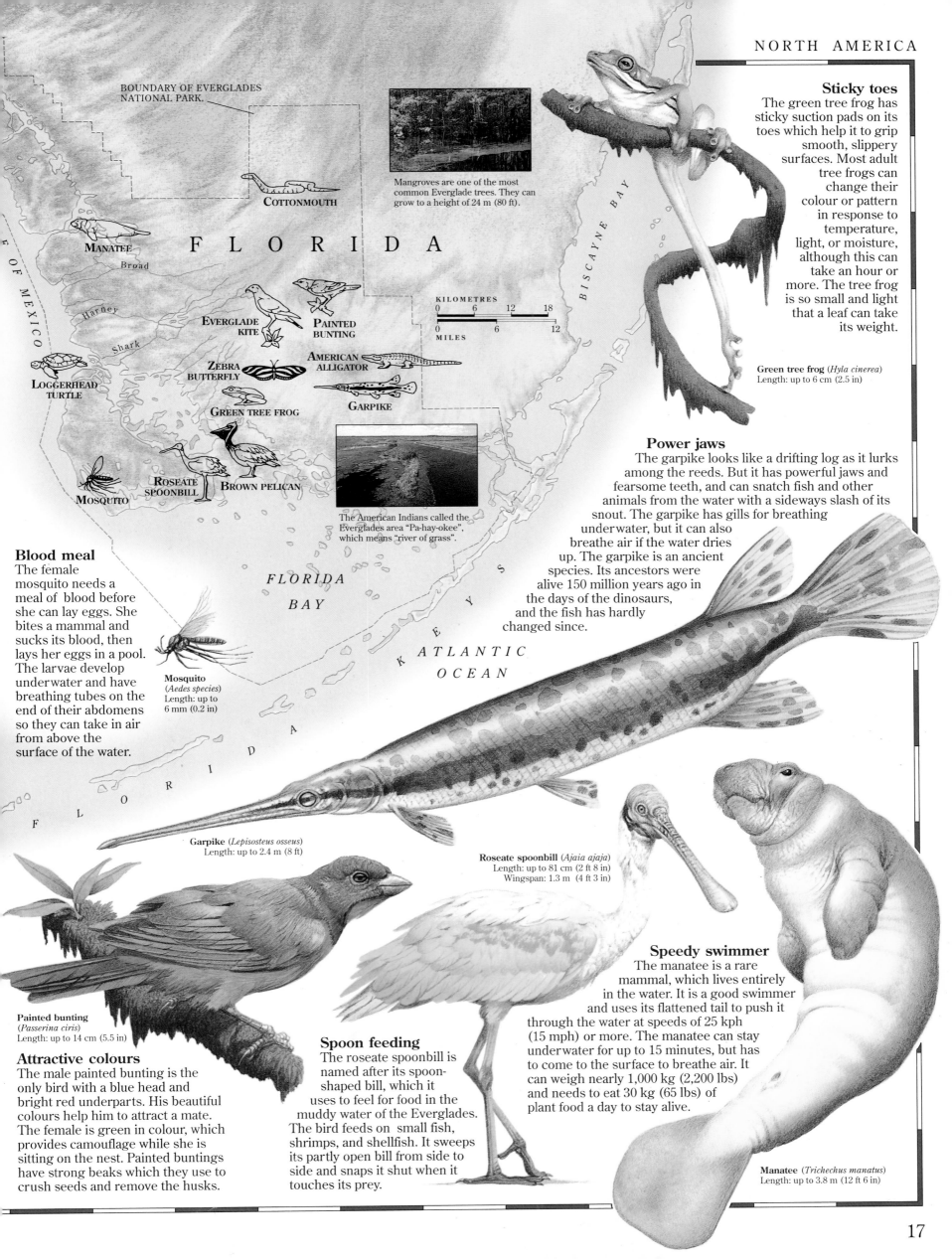

BOUNDARY OF EVERGLADES
NATIONAL PARK.

COTTONMOUTH

MANATEE

F L O R I D A

Broad

Harney

G F OF MEXICO

Shark

EVERGLADE
KITE

PAINTED
BUNTING

ZEBRA
BUTTERFLY

AMERICAN
ALLIGATOR

LOGGERHEAD
TURTLE

GREEN TREE FROG

GARPIKE

MOSQUITO

ROSEATE
SPOONBILL

BROWN PELICAN

Mangroves are one of the most common Everglade trees. They can grow to a height of 24 m (80 ft).

KILOMETRES
0   6   12   18
0   6   12
MILES

BISCAYNE BAY

The American Indians called the Everglades area "Pa-hay-okee", which means "river of grass".

F L O R I D A
B A Y

K E Y S

A T L A N T I C
O C E A N

F L O R I D A

Sticky toes
The green tree frog has sticky suction pads on its toes which help it to grip smooth, slippery surfaces. Most adult tree frogs can change their colour or pattern in response to temperature, light, or moisture, although this can take an hour or more. The tree frog is so small and light that a leaf can take its weight.

Green tree frog (*Hyla cinerea*)
Length: up to 6 cm (2.5 in)

Power jaws
The garpike looks like a drifting log as it lurks among the reeds. But it has powerful jaws and fearsome teeth, and can snatch fish and other animals from the water with a sideways slash of its snout. The garpike has gills for breathing underwater, but it can also breathe air if the water dries up. The garpike is an ancient species. Its ancestors were alive 150 million years ago in the days of the dinosaurs, and the fish has hardly changed since.

Blood meal
The female mosquito needs a meal of blood before she can lay eggs. She bites a mammal and sucks its blood, then lays her eggs in a pool. The larvae develop underwater and have breathing tubes on the end of their abdomens so they can take in air from above the surface of the water.

Mosquito
(*Aedes species*)
Length: up to 6 mm (0.2 in)

Garpike (*Lepisosteus osseus*)
Length: up to 2.4 m (8 ft)

Roseate spoonbill (*Ajaia ajaja*)
Length: up to 81 cm (2 ft 8 in)
Wingspan: 1.3 m (4 ft 3 in)

Painted bunting
(*Passerina ciris*)
Length: up to 14 cm (5.5 in)

Attractive colours
The male painted bunting is the only bird with a blue head and bright red underparts. His beautiful colours help him to attract a mate. The female is green in colour, which provides camouflage while she is sitting on the nest. Painted buntings have strong beaks which they use to crush seeds and remove the husks.

Spoon feeding
The roseate spoonbill is named after its spoon-shaped bill, which it uses to feel for food in the muddy water of the Everglades. The bird feeds on small fish, shrimps, and shellfish. It sweeps its partly open bill from side to side and snaps it shut when it touches its prey.

Speedy swimmer
The manatee is a rare mammal, which lives entirely in the water. It is a good swimmer and uses its flattened tail to push it through the water at speeds of 25 kph (15 mph) or more. The manatee can stay underwater for up to 15 minutes, but has to come to the surface to breathe air. It can weigh nearly 1,000 kg (2,200 lbs) and needs to eat 30 kg (65 lbs) of plant food a day to stay alive.

Manatee (*Trichechus manatus*)
Length: up to 3.8 m (12 ft 6 in)

Middle America

THE VARIED WILDLIFE of Central America and the islands of the Caribbean Sea reflects the many different habitats in the region. These range from mangrove swamps on the coasts, to grassland and rainforest inland. The climate in the area is warm all year round, but there are violent storms and hurricanes in the summer and autumn.

Central America forms an important land bridge along which animals can pass between North and South America. Although the Caribbean islands are close to Central America, the sea has prevented many animals from reaching them. Several unusual animals, such as the solenodon, have evolved on the islands, where they have few enemies or competitors.

Aerial acrobat
The kinkajou spends most of its life swinging like an acrobat in the tops of trees, using its tail to grip the branches. The kinkajou is also known as the honey bear because it often laps up the honey from bees' nests.

Thick vegetation covers the highland areas on the island of Jamaica.

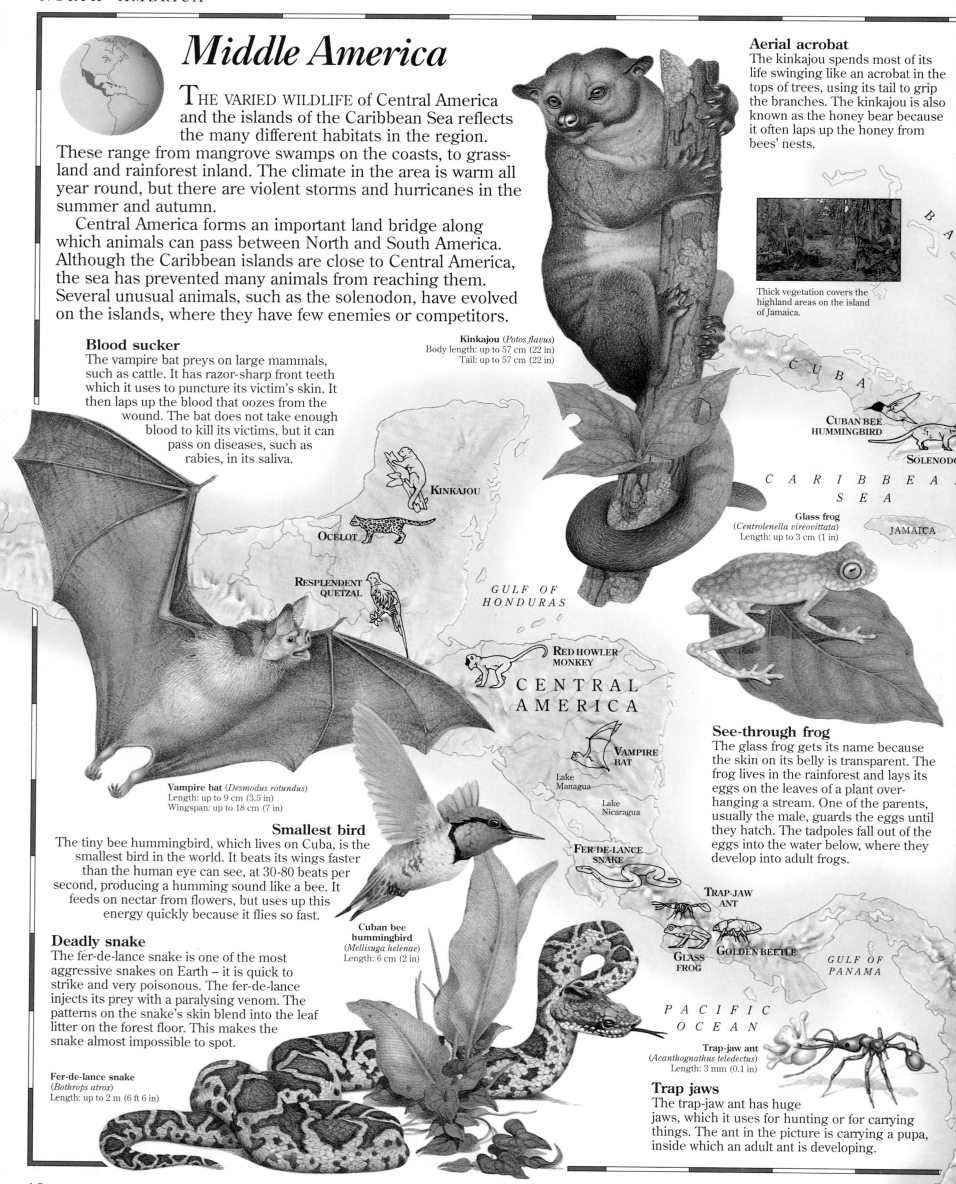

Kinkajou (*Potos flavus*)
Body length: up to 57 cm (22 in)
Tail: up to 57 cm (22 in)

Blood sucker
The vampire bat preys on large mammals, such as cattle. It has razor-sharp front teeth which it uses to puncture its victim's skin. It then laps up the blood that oozes from the wound. The bat does not take enough blood to kill its victims, but it can pass on diseases, such as rabies, in its saliva.

KINKAJOU

OCELOT

RESPLENDENT QUETZAL

GULF OF HONDURAS

RED HOWLER MONKEY

CENTRAL AMERICA

CUBA

CUBAN BEE HUMMINGBIRD

SOLENODON

CARIBBEAN SEA

JAMAICA

Glass frog
(*Centrolenella vireovittata*)
Length: up to 3 cm (1 in)

Vampire bat (*Desmodus rotundus*)
Length: up to 9 cm (3.5 in)
Wingspan: up to 18 cm (7 in)

VAMPIRE BAT

Lake Managua

Lake Nicaragua

FER-DE-LANCE SNAKE

Smallest bird
The tiny bee hummingbird, which lives on Cuba, is the smallest bird in the world. It beats its wings faster than the human eye can see, at 30-80 beats per second, producing a humming sound like a bee. It feeds on nectar from flowers, but uses up this energy quickly because it flies so fast.

Cuban bee hummingbird
(*Mellisuga helenae*)
Length: 6 cm (2 in)

See-through frog
The glass frog gets its name because the skin on its belly is transparent. The frog lives in the rainforest and lays its eggs on the leaves of a plant overhanging a stream. One of the parents, usually the male, guards the eggs until they hatch. The tadpoles fall out of the eggs into the water below, where they develop into adult frogs.

TRAP-JAW ANT

GLASS FROG

GOLDEN BEETLE

GULF OF PANAMA

Deadly snake
The fer-de-lance snake is one of the most aggressive snakes on Earth – it is quick to strike and very poisonous. The fer-de-lance injects its prey with a paralysing venom. The patterns on the snake's skin blend into the leaf litter on the forest floor. This makes the snake almost impossible to spot.

PACIFIC OCEAN

Trap-jaw ant
(*Acanthognathus teledectus*)
Length: 3 mm (0.1 in)

Fer-de-lance snake
(*Bothrops atrox*)
Length: up to 2 m (6 ft 6 in)

Trap jaws
The trap-jaw ant has huge jaws, which it uses for hunting or for carrying things. The ant in the picture is carrying a pupa, inside which an adult ant is developing.

Spotted cat

The beautiful ocelot has become very rare because its forest home is being destroyed, and because it is hunted for its fur. Each cat has a different pattern of markings on its coat. The ocelot is an excellent climber and swimmer. It comes out at night to hunt for birds, snakes and small mammals.

Rare animal

The solenodon is a rare animal found only on the island of Cuba. It is related to the hedgehog. The solenodon is in danger of becoming extinct because it reproduces slowly. It is also threatened by new species, such as the mongoose, which humans have introduced to Cuba.

Ocelot
(*Felis pardalis*)
Body length: up to
1.3 m (4 ft 3 in)
Tail: up to 40 cm (15 in)

Solenodon (*Solenodon cubanus*)
Body length: up to 32 cm (13 in)
Tail: up to 25 cm (10 in)

HISPANIOLA   PUERTO RICO

Sacred bird

The ancient peoples of Central America once worshipped the brilliantly coloured quetzal as the god of the air. They used the male bird's long tail feathers in their religious ceremonies. The male sheds his tail feathers after each breeding season and grows new ones the following year.

Resplendent quetzal
(*Pharomachrus mocinno*)
Body length: up to
20 cm (8 in)
Tail: up to 60 cm (2 ft)

Loudest animal

Male red howler monkeys are the noisiest land animals in the world. They shout and roar at rival monkeys to tell them to keep out of their territory. The red howler has a large voice box which enables it to roar so loudly that it can be heard up to 3 km (2 miles) away.

Red howler monkey
(*Alouatta seniculus*)
Body length: up to
90 cm (3 ft)
Tail: up to
90 cm (3 ft)

GUADELOUPE

Golden beetle
(*Plusiotis
resplendens*)
Length: up to
4 cm (1.5 in)

Shiny wings

The metallic sheen on the wing cases of the golden beetle acts as a form of camouflage. The wing cases reflect the light and make it hard for enemies to see the beetle's outline.

MARTINIQUE

BARBADOS

ST VINCENT
PARROT

SCARLET IBIS

TRINIDAD

Many of the islands were formed by underwater volcanoes. There are still active volcanoes in the region.

St Vincent parrot
(*Amazona guildingii*)
Length: 40 cm (15 in)
Wingspan: 63 cm (2 ft)

Handy feet

This parrot lives only on the Caribbean island of St Vincent. Parrots have unusual feet, with two toes pointing forwards and two pointing backwards. This gives them a powerful grip on branches and allows them to use their feet like hands. Each parrot is either right- or left-footed.

SOUTH AMERICA

Many of the Caribbean islands have beautiful, sandy beaches and are popular holiday resorts.

KILOMETRES
0   100   200   300

0   100   200
MILES

Scarlet ibis
(*Eudocimus ruber*)
Length: 64 cm (2 ft 1 in)
Wingspan: 89 cm (2 ft 11 in)

Curved bill

The scarlet ibis has a long, curved bill which it uses to probe in soft mud for insects, crustaceans, frogs, and fishes. Ibises feed and nest in flocks. They often nest in trees or in areas surrounded by water, where they are safer from enemies. The island of Trinidad is famous for its nesting colonies.

The Galápagos

THE GALÁPAGOS ISLANDS lie in the Pacific Ocean, about 1,000 km (600 miles) west of South America. The Galápagos are home to a great variety of unique and unusual animals, which originally swam, flew, or drifted across to the islands from the Americas. Few mammals managed this crossing, so the islands are dominated by birds and reptiles, such as iguanas and giant tortoises. In fact the word "Galápagos" comes from a Spanish name for the tortoise.

In 1835 the British naturalist, Charles Darwin, visited the Galápagos. He noticed slight differences between animals of the same kind which lived on different islands. From this he came to believe that over many generations animals change, or evolve, to suit their habitat. He developed his findings into a theory of evolution, which is still accepted by many people today.

Useless wings

The flightless cormorant probably flew to the Galápagos. It has since lost the power of flight, because it had no enemies to escape from before people settled on the islands. Its wings are only one-third of the size they would have to be to support it in flight. The cormorant dives underwater to catch fish. Its feathers are not waterproof, so after diving the bird has to spread out its wings in the sun to dry them.

Flightless cormorant
(*Nannopterum harrisi*)
Length: 1 m (3 ft 3 in)

ISLA PINTA

ISLA GENOVESA

ISLA MARCHENA

FLIGHTLESS CORMORANT

Wolf Volcano

Underwater volcanoes formed the Galápagos Islands, which are made of volcanic lava.

Darwin Volcano

GALÁPAGOS PENGUIN

ISLA FERNANDINA

La Cumbre Volcano

LAND IGUANA

Alcedo Volcano

The smaller Galápagos Islands are largely waterless and few plants can survive.

SALLYLIGHTFOOT CRAB

ISLA SAN SALVADOR

The prickly pear is one of the few plants that can grow on the lava fields.

PACIFIC OCEAN

GALÁPAGOS FUR SEAL

ISLA SANTA CRUZ

WOODPECKER FINCH

VERMILION FLYCATCHER

GIANT TORTOISE

I S L A

I S A B E L A

Santo Tomás Volcano

ISLA SANTA FÉ

Land iguana
(*Conolophus subcristatus*)
Length: over 1 m (3 ft 3 in)

MARINE IGUANA

KILOMETRES
0   5   10   15   20

0   5   10   15
MILES

Fearless footwork

Large numbers of sallylightfoot crabs live on the rocky shores of the Galápagos. The crab has a hard shell for protection. As it grows, it sheds its shell from time to time and grows a larger one. The crab usually runs sideways to avoid tripping over its own legs. Its front legs have developed into a pair of pincers for grasping food.

Sallylightfoot crab
(*Grapsus grapsus*)
Width of shell: 15 cm (6 in)

ISLA SANTA MARÍA

Fighting males

During the mating season, the male land iguana defends his territory against other males. If a rival approaches, he bobs his head in a ritual display to warn the intruder to keep away. If this does not work, a fight may break out, with the iguanas trying to bite each other with their strong teeth. They rarely fight to the death though, and the weaker male usually retreats when he realizes he cannot win.

Sea lizard

The marine iguana is the only lizard in the world that swims and feeds in the sea. It has a short snout, which enables it to gnaw seaweed off underwater rocks. Its strong claws help it to grip the slippery rocks.

Marine iguana
(*Amblyrhynchus cristatus*)
Length: over 1 m (3 ft 3 in)

Trusty tools

Unusually, the woodpecker finch uses a tool to help it find food. This bird feeds on insect grubs, which live under the bark or inside the trunks of trees. It uses a small twig or cactus spine to dig them out. The woodpecker finch may even make the tool itself by breaking a twig to the right length.

Woodpecker finch
(*Camarhynchus pallidus*)
Length: 15 cm (6 in)

Pirate of the air

The frigate bird is named after a ship called a frigate, which was often used by pirates. When it sees another bird carrying food, the frigate bird flies after it and forces it to drop the food. Then it swoops down and grabs the stolen food in mid-air. During courtship, the male frigate bird puffs out his red throat pouch to attract a female.

**Magnificent
frigate bird**
(*Fregata magnificens*)
Length: 1 m (3 ft 3 in)
Wingspan: up to
2.4 m (8 ft)

Blue-footed booby
(*Sula nebouxii*)
Length: 86 cm
(2 ft 10 in)
Wingspan: up to
1.7 m (5 ft 8 in)

Blue shoes

The blue-footed booby lifts its feet up and down in a comical courtship dance. The name "booby" comes from the Spanish word *bobo*, meaning "clown". The booby feeds on fish, which it catches underwater in its long, jagged bill. It often plunges into the sea from a great height to catch fish.

Fur coats

The Galápagos fur seal has a thick fur coat, which consists of an outer layer of long guard hairs and an inner layer of soft underfur. These seals were hunted almost to extinction for their skins, which were made into fur coats for people. They are now a protected species and their numbers are beginning to increase.

Galápagos fur seal
(*Arctocephalus galapagoensis*)
Length: up to 1.8 m (5 ft 10 in)

**MAGNIFICENT
FRIGATE BIRD**

**ISLA SAN
CRISTÓBAL**

Unique penguin

The Galápagos penguin is the only penguin found on the Equator. Most other penguins live in Antarctica. It can survive in the Galápagos because of a water current which sweeps past the islands, carrying cold water from the Antarctic.

Galápagos penguin
(*Spheniscus mendiculus*)
Height: 53 cm (21 in)

Fly catcher

The vermilion flycatcher often perches on the back of a giant tortoise so that it can snap up flies disturbed by the tortoise's feet. The male bird has bright red feathers, which he shows off by flying overhead in a display to attract a mate.

Vermilion flycatcher
(*Pyrocephalus rubinus*)
Length: 15 cm (6 in)

**BLUE-FOOTED
BOOBY**

ISLA ESPAÑOLA

Super shells

The Galápagos are home to several different species of giant tortoise, which live on different islands. Each species has developed a slightly differently shaped shell to suit its habitat and diet. Giant tortoises have been able to survive on the islands because they can go for long periods without food or water and can move easily over rough ground. A giant tortoise may live to be more than 100 years old.

Giant tortoise
(*Geochelone elephantopus*)
Shell length: 1.2 m (4 ft)

21

The Andes

THE ANDES are the longest chain of mountains in the world. They stretch right down the western side of South America, from the Caribbean Sea in the north to Cape Horn in the south. The Andes are some of the youngest mountains on Earth. Many of the mountains in the range are volcanic, and some of them are active. Below the peaks of the Andes lie high plateaus, studded with lakes. To the east, the land slopes gently downwards to the grasslands of the pampas and the rainforests of the Amazon basin.

Animals that live in these mountains have to cope with the thin air found at high altitudes. Some of them have developed extra-large hearts and lungs to help them get enough oxygen from the air. The temperature in the Andes drops to around -10°C (14°F) at night, so animals such as the vicuna and alpaca have thick coats to keep them warm.

Wide wings

The Andean condor is one of the largest flying birds that has ever lived. It has huge wings and can soar and glide for long distances. The condor eats the flesh of dead animals. Its head and neck are bald, so it can reach into a carcass without dirtying any feathers.

Andean condor
(*Vultur gryphus*)
Wingspan: up to 3 m (10 ft)

Whistling guard

Most vicunas live in a small family group, which is fiercely guarded by an adult male. If the male spots any sign of danger, he whistles loudly to give the alarm so that the females and young can escape.Vicunas can run at speeds of up to 47 kph (29 mph) over long distances.

Digging bird

The dark-faced ground tyrant digs a long underground burrow with a nesting chamber at the end. The bird uses its beak as a pickaxe and clears away the soil with its sharp claws. The ground tyrant runs quickly along the mountain slopes on its long legs, snatching insects from the ground.

Pudu
(*Pudu mephistopheles*)
Body length:
65 cm (2 ft 2 in)

Dark-faced ground tyrant
(*Muscisaxicola macloviana*)
Length: 15 cm (6 in)
Wingspan: 21 cm (8 in)

Vicuna
(*Vicugna vicugna*)
Height at shoulder: up to 1 m (3 ft 3 in)
Body length: up to 1.6 m (5 ft 2 in)

Smallest deer

The pudu is the smallest deer on the American continent. It is only 40 cm (15 in) high. The pudu lives in remote areas of the mountain lowlands and is very shy. This makes it hard to observe and very little is known about its behaviour. It probably lives in small groups and feeds on leaves, shoots, and fruit.

Frogs in the throat

The male Darwin's frog carries his tadpoles in huge pouches in his throat. This keeps them safe from enemies. While the tadpoles are in his throat, the frog can make only a faint call. After about three weeks, the tadpoles change into tiny froglets and the male spits them out. The female frog plays no part in rearing the young.

Darwin's frog
(*Rhinoderma darwinii*)
Length: up to 3 cm (1 in)

Handy nose

The Andean tapir lives in the mountain forests. Its snout and upper lip are joined together to form a short trunk. It uses this as a nose and as an extra hand to tear leaves off branches. Tapirs are hunted by many other animals, including the jaguar, and must always be on the look out for danger.

Andean tapir
(*Tapirus pinchaque*)
Body length: 2 m (6 ft 6 in)

Biggest hummingbird

The Andean giant hummingbird is the largest hummingbird in the world. During the cold mountain nights, its body temperature falls to just above freezing point. This helps the bird to save energy, which it would otherwise use to keep its body warm.

Giant hummingbird
(*Patagona gigas*)
Length: 21 cm (8.5 in)

Chiselling beak

The Andean flicker is a type of woodpecker. It uses its strong beak to chisel out a nesting hole in the spiny leaves of a Puya plant. The flicker's feet are specially adapted for climbing, with two toes pointing forwards and two backwards. Its claws are curved for extra grip.

Andean flicker
(*Colaptes rupicola*)
Length: 30 cm (12 in)

Furry coat

Chinchillas live high up in the Andes and have soft, thick fur coats to keep out the cold. Many chinchillas have been killed for their fur, which is used to make coats and jackets, and they are now rare animals. Chinchillas make their homes in holes and cracks among the rocks.

Chinchilla (*Chinchilla laniger*)
Body length: up to 38 cm (15 in)
Tail: up to 15 cm (6 in)

Changing spectacles

The white markings around the eyes of the spectacled bear make it look as if it is wearing spectacles. These markings vary a lot, and each animal has different-shaped spectacles. The bear is a good climber. At night it sleeps in a tree, where it builds a rough nest of sticks.

Spectacled bear (*Tremarctos ornatus*)
Height at shoulder: 75 cm (2 ft 6 in)
Body length: up to 1.8 m (5 ft 10 in)

Alpaca (*Lama pacos*)
Height at shoulder: 1.2 m (4 ft)

Waterfall duck

The torrent duck feeds in the fast-flowing streams of the Andes, where there are many waterfalls and rapids. It uses its sharp claws to grip slippery boulders and steers its way through the rushing waters, using its stiff tail as a rudder. Its streamlined body shape helps it to swim underwater when it dives to look for food.

Shaggy camel

The alpaca is a relative of the camel. It has a shaggy coat of fine, soft hair that reaches almost to the ground. People farm alpacas like sheep, cutting off their woolly coats to make clothes. An alpaca's fleece weighs about 3 kg (6.5 lbs).

Torrent duck
(*Merganetta armata*)
Length: 43 cm (17 in)

SOUTH AMERICA

Amazon

ANDEAN CONDOR

AMAZON BASIN

The Andes range contains 50 peaks that are over 6,000 m (19,700 ft) high.

GROUND TYRANT

SPECTACLED BEAR

Lake Titicaca

A variety of birds and animals live in the rushes around Lake Titicaca and feed in the lake itself.

CHINCHILLA

DARWIN'S FROG

VICUNA

TORRENT DUCK

ANDEAN TAPIR

ALPACA

GIANT HUMMINGBIRD

PACIFIC OCEAN

Salado

Paraná

ANDEAN FLICKER

PAMPAS

Colorado

PUDU

Parinacota is one of the many active volcanoes in the Andes.

ATLANTIC OCEAN

FALKLAND ISLANDS

TIERRA DEL FUEGO

PATAGONIA

CAPE HORN

KILOMETRES
0   200   400   600

0   200   400
MILES

23

Amazon Rainforest

THE VAST AMAZON JUNGLE is the largest area of tropical rainforest in the world. It covers about 7,000,000 sq km (2,702,700 sq miles) – an area 12 times the size of France. The rainforest is situated in the huge basin of the Amazon River, which flows 6,450 km (4,000 miles) across South America. The weather in the Amazon basin is hot and humid all year round.

The Amazon rainforest is home to a greater variety of wildlife than anywhere else on Earth. Many animals live in the treetops, where there are plenty of leaves, flowers, and fruit to feed on. Animals such as the spider monkey have grasping tails and long claws to help them swing through the branches; others have flaps of skin that unfold like wings as they glide from branch to branch. Rainforest birds such as parrots have short, broad wings that allow them to fly through the trees. On the forest floor, many animals find food with their long noses and sharp digging claws. Today large areas of the rainforest are being cleared for farming and mining, and many of the animals and plants are threatened.

Reflecting wings
The male morpho butterfly is brilliantly coloured because of the way the tiny scales on its wings reflect the light. As the butterfly moves its wings, the colours change. Many morphos have been collected for jewellery or decoration, and they are in danger of becoming extinct.

Blue morpho butterfly
(*Morpho rhetenor*)
Wingspan: up to 18 cm (7 in)

Toco toucan
(*Ramphastos toco*)
Length: 60 cm (2 ft)
Bill: 25 cm (10 in)

Biggest bill
The toco toucan has the biggest bill of any toucan. But its bill is lighter than it looks. Both parts are hollow, with thin rods of bone inside for support. With its long bill, the toucan can reach fruit on twigs too thin to bear its weight.

Underwater danger
The caiman is a type of crocodile. It lurks underwater with just its nose and eyes showing. When a thirsty animal comes for a drink, the caiman snaps it up with its sharp teeth and holds it underwater until it drowns.

Spectacled caiman
(*Caiman crocodylus*)
Length including tail:
up to 4.5 m (15 ft)

Hoatzin
(*Opisthocomus hoatzin*)
Length: up to 66 cm
(2 ft 2 in)

Weak wings
The hoatzin has such weak flight muscles that it cannot fly more than 100 m (330 ft) or so before it has to crash-land for a rest. It uses its wings and tail for extra support as it climbs through the trees. Young hoatzins have little claws on their wings to help them climb.

Acrobatic leaps
The spider monkey is an amazing acrobat. It makes leaps of 10 m (33 ft) or more through the trees, using its tail like an extra hand or foot. This type of tail is called prehensile. Underneath its tail is a patch of ridged skin, which helps it to get a firm grip on the branches.

Spider monkey
(*Ateles geoffroyi*)
Body length:
up to 60 cm (2 ft)
Tail: up to 90 cm (3 ft)

Jaguar (*Panthera onca*)
Height to shoulder: 71 cm (2 ft 4 in)
Body length: up to 1.7 m (5 ft 9 in)

Spotted cat
The jaguar is the largest cat in South America. Unlike the leopard, it has black marks inside each ring of spots. Its coat acts as camouflage in the forest, and it can creep up on the animals it hunts without being seen.

CARIBBE

Lak
Maracaib

GULF
OF
PANAMA

The highest parts of the rain forest receive 305 cm (120 in) of rain each year.

HARPY EAGLE

SLOTH

SCARLET MACAW

PACIFIC OCEAN

A N D E S   M T S

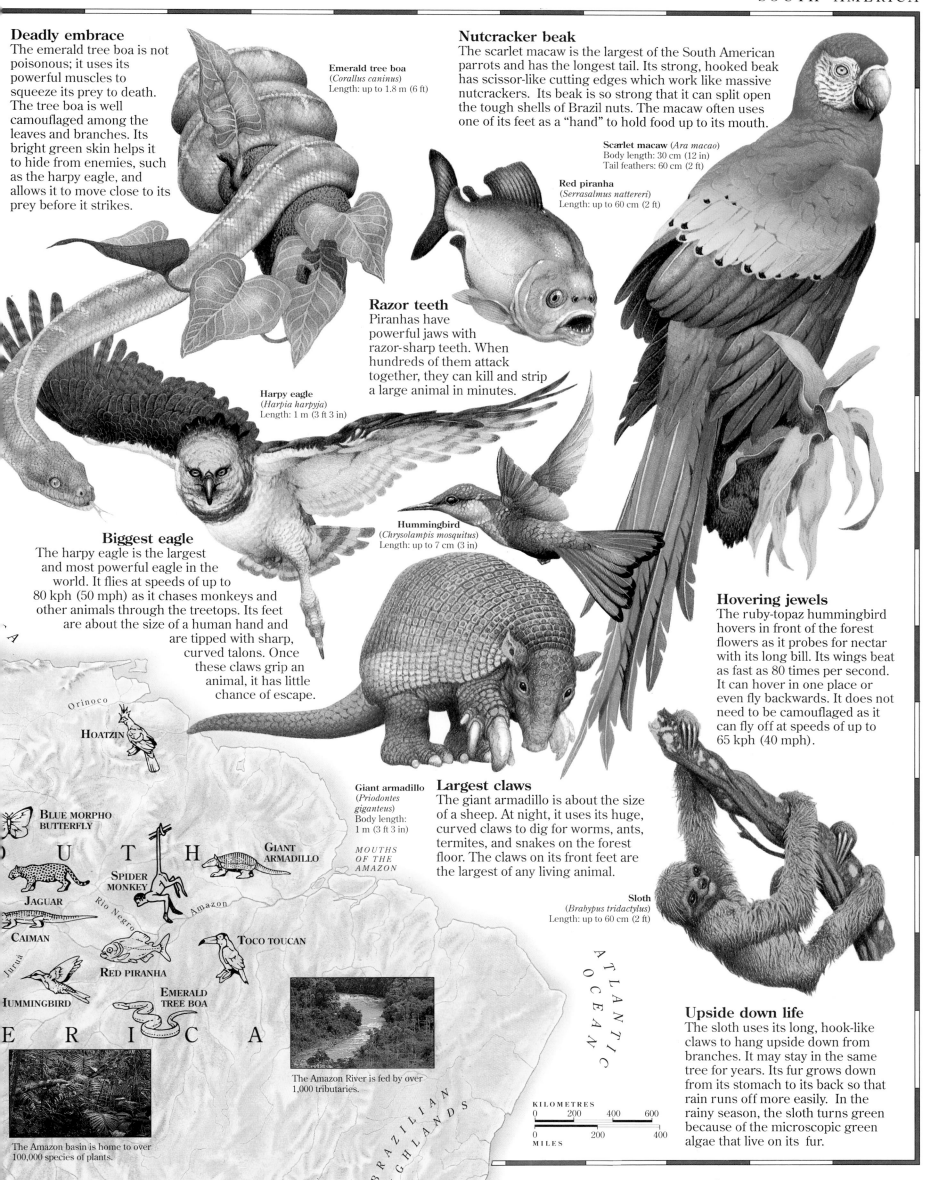

Deadly embrace
The emerald tree boa is not poisonous; it uses its powerful muscles to squeeze its prey to death. The tree boa is well camouflaged among the leaves and branches. Its bright green skin helps it to hide from enemies, such as the harpy eagle, and allows it to move close to its prey before it strikes.

Emerald tree boa
(*Corallus caninus*)
Length: up to 1.8 m (6 ft)

Nutcracker beak
The scarlet macaw is the largest of the South American parrots and has the longest tail. Its strong, hooked beak has scissor-like cutting edges which work like massive nutcrackers. Its beak is so strong that it can split open the tough shells of Brazil nuts. The macaw often uses one of its feet as a "hand" to hold food up to its mouth.

Scarlet macaw (*Ara macao*)
Body length: 30 cm (12 in)
Tail feathers: 60 cm (2 ft)

Red piranha
(*Serrasalmus nattereri*)
Length: up to 60 cm (2 ft)

Razor teeth
Piranhas have powerful jaws with razor-sharp teeth. When hundreds of them attack together, they can kill and strip a large animal in minutes.

Harpy eagle
(*Harpia harpyja*)
Length: 1 m (3 ft 3 in)

Biggest eagle
The harpy eagle is the largest and most powerful eagle in the world. It flies at speeds of up to 80 kph (50 mph) as it chases monkeys and other animals through the treetops. Its feet are about the size of a human hand and are tipped with sharp, curved talons. Once these claws grip an animal, it has little chance of escape.

Hummingbird
(*Chrysolampis mosquitus*)
Length: up to 7 cm (3 in)

Hovering jewels
The ruby-topaz hummingbird hovers in front of the forest flowers as it probes for nectar with its long bill. Its wings beat as fast as 80 times per second. It can hover in one place or even fly backwards. It does not need to be camouflaged as it can fly off at speeds of up to 65 kph (40 mph).

Giant armadillo
(*Priodontes giganteus*)
Body length:
1 m (3 ft 3 in)

MOUTHS OF THE AMAZON

Largest claws
The giant armadillo is about the size of a sheep. At night, it uses its huge, curved claws to dig for worms, ants, termites, and snakes on the forest floor. The claws on its front feet are the largest of any living animal.

Sloth
(*Brabypus tridactylus*)
Length: up to 60 cm (2 ft)

Upside down life
The sloth uses its long, hook-like claws to hang upside down from branches. It may stay in the same tree for years. Its fur grows down from its stomach to its back so that rain runs off more easily. In the rainy season, the sloth turns green because of the microscopic green algae that live on its fur.

Orinoco

HOATZIN

BLUE MORPHO BUTTERFLY

GIANT ARMADILLO

JAGUAR

SPIDER MONKEY

Rio Negro

Amazon

CAIMAN

Jurúa

RED PIRANHA

TOCO TOUCAN

HUMMINGBIRD

EMERALD TREE BOA

The Amazon River is fed by over 1,000 tributaries.

ATLANTIC OCEAN

E   R   I   C   A

The Amazon basin is home to over 100,000 species of plants.

BRAZILIAN HIGHLANDS

KILOMETRES
0   200   400   600
0   200   400
MILES

Titicaca

25

The Pampas

THE PAMPAS IS A VAST GRASSY plain which covers an area of almost 777,000 sq km (300,000 sq miles) in South America. The climate in the pampas is generally dry. Although grasses flourish in these conditions, trees and larger plants can only survive along river banks. Termite mounds, which can be up to 2 m (6 ft 6 in) high, dot the pampas plain.

Many pampas animals, such as the armadillo, live in underground burrows. This protects them from fires, which are common on the dry grassland. Much of the pampas is now used by farmers for grazing cattle. Many of the wild animals therefore face extra competition for food, and some species are declining as a result.

Speedy sprinter
The rhea is a flightless bird. It can run at speeds of more than 50 kph (30 mph). The male rhea rears the chicks and defends the nest. He will attack anything that comes too close, even people or small aeroplanes.

Grey rhea
(*Rhea americana*)
Height: up to 1.5 m (5 ft)

Long jump
The mara, or Patagonian hare, has long back legs which it uses to bound away from danger. It can cover up to 2 m (6 ft 6 in) in one leap. Although the mara looks rather like a hare, it is in fact related to the guinea pig. Maras live in burrows, in groups of up to 40 animals.

Mara (*Dolichotis patagona*)
Body length: up to 75 cm (2 ft 6 in)

Baker bird
The ovenbird is named after its nest, which looks like a round earthenware oven. There are few trees on the pampas, so the nest is often situated on a post instead. The female bird builds the nest from up to 2,500 lumps of mud.

Pink fairy armadillo
(*Chlamyphorus truncatus*)
Body length: up to 15 cm (6 in)

Rare deer
The pampas deer is one of the few large plant-eating animals left on the grasslands. It is now rare, due to hunting and competition from cattle grazing. The male has glands on his hooves which give off a smell that can be detected more than 1.5 km (1 mile) away.

Ovenbird
(*Furnarius rufus*)
Length: up to 20 cm (8 in)

Chain mail
The pink fairy armadillo has protective armour on its back, made of plates of bone covered with horny scales. It uses the huge claws on its front feet for digging. Because it spends a lot of time underground, the armadillo's eyes are tiny and its sight is poor.

Bullying bird
The crested caracara is a bird of prey. It eats insects and other small animals, but it also likes carrion (the flesh of dead animals). The caracara sometimes pecks and bullies a vulture until it forces it to cough up some of the carrion it has just eaten.

Crested caracara (*Polyborus plancus*)
Length: up to 60 cm (2 ft)

Viscacha (*Lagostomus maximus*)
Body length: up to 66 cm (2 ft 2 in)
Tail: up to 20 cm (8 in)

Pampas deer
(*Odocoileus bezoarticus*)
Height at shoulder: 70 cm (2 ft 3 in)

Underground city
Viscachas are rodents that dig huge networks of tunnels under the pampas. Many generations of viscachas may live in the same burrow. Other animals, such as maras and burrowing owls, often live in viscacha burrows. The viscacha digs mainly with its front feet, pushing the soil out of the way with its nose. It can close its nostrils to stop soil getting in.

SOUTH AMERICA

GIANT ANTEATER

MANED WOLF

PINK FAIRY ARMADILLO

CAVY

OVENBIRD

GRAY RHEA

VISCACHA

MARA

CRESTED TINAMOU

PAMPAS

BURROWING OWL

PAMPAS DEER

CRESTED CARACARA

Some pampas grasses can grow to a height of 2.5 m (8 ft).

The lack of trees and bushes on the pampas means that many animals and birds have to take cover in underground burrows.

Today large areas of the pampas are used by farmers for raising beef cattle.

Camouflage colours

The mottled patterns on the crested tinamou's feathers help to camouflage it on the open grasslands. The tinamou has powerful legs and can run fast for short distances, but soon becomes tired. It is not good at flying and often collides with obstacles. The bird lays brightly coloured eggs in a hollow on the ground.

Crested tinamou
(*Eudromia elegans*)
Length: up to 53 cm (21 in)

Long-legged wolf

The maned wolf has long legs which enable it to move easily through the long grass of the pampas. If a maned wolf is threatened by an enemy, the mane of hair on its neck and shoulders stands up to make it look bigger and more frightening. It hunts at night, for small mammals, birds, reptiles, and insects.

Maned wolf
(*Chrysocyon brachyurus*)
Body length: 1.2 m (4 ft)
Tail: 30 cm (12 in)

Sharp claws

The cavy is the wild ancestor of the guinea pig that some people keep as a pet. The cavy has sharp claws and is a good digger, but it often prefers to use burrows made by other animals or to shelter under rocks. Cavies usually live in small groups but sometimes hundreds of them may live together in a suitable area.

Cavy (*Cavia aperez*)
Body length: up to 40 cm (16 in)

Terrific tongue

The giant anteater feeds on ants and termites which it licks up with its long, sticky tongue. A giant anteater may have to visit 40 termite mounds in one hour to find enough food to eat. It rips open the mounds with its huge claws. The anteater sleeps in the open and wraps its hairy tail over its body like a blanket.

Burrowing owl (*Speotyto cunicularia*)
Length: 20 cm (8 in)

Giant anteater
(*Myrmecophaga tridactyla*)
Body length: up to 1.2 m (4 ft)
Tail: up to 90 cm (3 ft)

Daytime owl

Unlike most other owls, the burrowing owl hunts during the day. It perches on the mounds of soil dug out by viscachas, watching for insects or other small animals to stir in the grass. Its long legs help it to run fast over the ground and catch its food. This owl nests in an underground burrow.

27

Conifer Forests

A THICK BAND OF DENSE EVERGREEN FOREST stretches across the northern parts of Europe, covering large areas of Scotland and Scandinavia. There are smaller evergreen forests farther south, such as the Black Forest in Germany and the Ardennes in Belgium. The most common trees in these forests are conifers (trees that have cones), such as pines, spruces, and firs. A thick layer of needles usually covers the ground. In recent years acid rain, which is especially harmful to trees with needle-like leaves, has damaged many European conifer forests.

Animals that live in these forests have to survive in a severe climate. The winters are bitterly cold, but most conifer trees keep their leaves all year round and provide some shelter from the worst of the weather. Some forest animals, such as the stoat, grow white coats in the winter so that they are camouflaged against the snow. Other animals, such as the long-eared bat and the wood ant, hibernate during the winter months to avoid the worst of the weather, while some birds, such as the osprey, migrate south to warmer countries.

Fish snatcher
The osprey feeds on fish which it snatches from lakes. It has long, sharp claws and horny spines under its toes which enable it to grip a slippery fish. An adult osprey can carry a fish weighing up to 2 kg (4.5 lbs). In autumn, the osprey migrates to Africa where the weather is warmer and there are plenty of fish for it to eat.

Osprey (*Pandion haliaetus*)
Length: up to 62 cm (2 ft)
Wingspan: up to 1.6 m (5 ft 4 in)

Long-eared owl
(*Asio otus*)
Length: 34 cm (13 in)
Wingspan: 95 cm (3 ft 1 in)

Long ears
The long-eared bat's huge ears are three-quarters the length of its body. They are so big that a young bat cannot hold its ears up straight until it is old enough to fly. The bat feeds on moths, midges, and flies, often swooping down to pick them off plants. During the cold winter months, the long-eared bat usually hibernates in a cave.

Long-eared bat
(*Plecotus auritus*)
Body length: up to 5 cm (2 in)
Wingspan: up to 28 cm (11 in)

Underground city
Wood ants build huge nests on the forest floor from pine needles and other plant material. The nests help to keep the ants warm in winter, when they hibernate in the soil beneath the mound. If it is threatened, a wood ant sprays its enemy with a stinging liquid called formic acid from glands on its abdomen. People can see and smell this chemical. The wood ant eats all kinds of other insects and may catch some of them high up in the trees.

Wood ant (*Formica rufa*)
Length: 1 cm (0.5 in)

False ears
The "ears" of the long-eared owl are only tufts of feathers. Its real ear openings are on the sides of its head. The owl hunts at night using its sharp eyesight and good hearing to find small mammals on the woodland floor.

Wild cat (*Felis sylvestris*)
Body length: up to 75 cm (2 ft 6 in)
Tail: up to 37 cm (15 in)

Common crossbill
(*Loxia curvirostra*)
Length: 16 cm (6.5 in)

Crossed beak
The crossbill uses its chunky, crossed beak to tear open pine cones. Then it licks out the seeds with its horny tongue. Adult crossbills regurgitate partly digested seeds to feed their young. Every few years, crossbills move out of their normal breeding areas and invade other parts of Europe in enormous numbers. If conditions are favourable, they may settle in the new area for one or more seasons.

Stripey tail
The wild cat is closely related to the domestic cat, but it is slightly bigger, and has a thicker tail with black rings on it. The wild cat hunts at night for small mammals, birds, and insects. The forests provide it with cover for hunting.

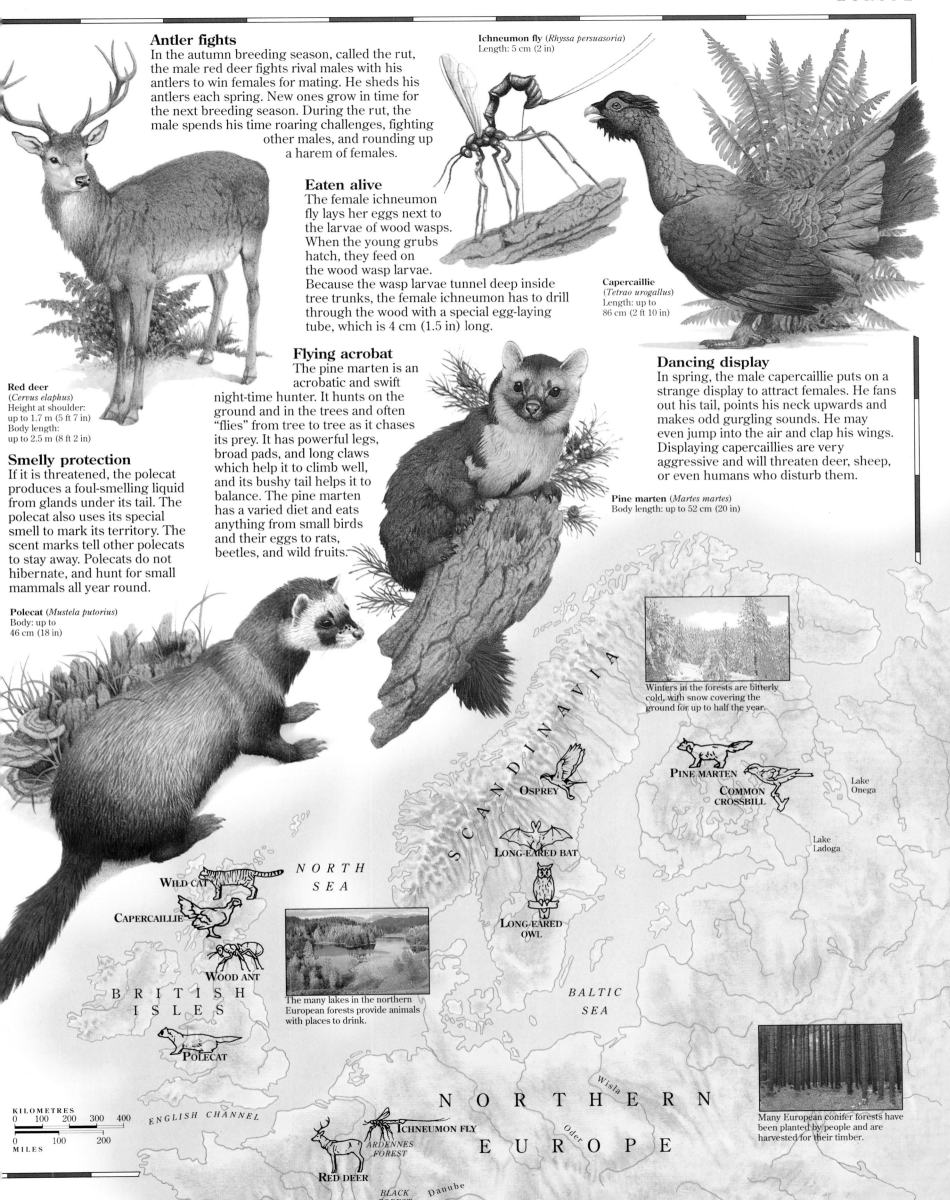

Antler fights

In the autumn breeding season, called the rut, the male red deer fights rival males with his antlers to win females for mating. He sheds his antlers each spring. New ones grow in time for the next breeding season. During the rut, the male spends his time roaring challenges, fighting other males, and rounding up a harem of females.

Ichneumon fly (*Rhyssa persuasoria*)
Length: 5 cm (2 in)

Eaten alive

The female ichneumon fly lays her eggs next to the larvae of wood wasps. When the young grubs hatch, they feed on the wood wasp larvae. Because the wasp larvae tunnel deep inside tree trunks, the female ichneumon has to drill through the wood with a special egg-laying tube, which is 4 cm (1.5 in) long.

Capercaillie
(*Tetrao urogallus*)
Length: up to
86 cm (2 ft 10 in)

Red deer
(*Cervus elaphus*)
Height at shoulder:
up to 1.7 m (5 ft 7 in)
Body length:
up to 2.5 m (8 ft 2 in)

Smelly protection

If it is threatened, the polecat produces a foul-smelling liquid from glands under its tail. The polecat also uses its special smell to mark its territory. The scent marks tell other polecats to stay away. Polecats do not hibernate, and hunt for small mammals all year round.

Polecat (*Mustela putorius*)
Body: up to
46 cm (18 in)

Flying acrobat

The pine marten is an acrobatic and swift night-time hunter. It hunts on the ground and in the trees and often "flies" from tree to tree as it chases its prey. It has powerful legs, broad pads, and long claws which help it to climb well, and its bushy tail helps it to balance. The pine marten has a varied diet and eats anything from small birds and their eggs to rats, beetles, and wild fruits.

Pine marten (*Martes martes*)
Body length: up to 52 cm (20 in)

Dancing display

In spring, the male capercaillie puts on a strange display to attract females. He fans out his tail, points his neck upwards and makes odd gurgling sounds. He may even jump into the air and clap his wings. Displaying capercaillies are very aggressive and will threaten deer, sheep, or even humans who disturb them.

Winters in the forests are bitterly cold, with snow covering the ground for up to half the year.

SCANDINAVIA

OSPREY

PINE MARTEN

COMMON CROSSBILL

Lake Onega

LONG-EARED BAT

Lake Ladoga

LONG-EARED OWL

WILD CAT

CAPERCAILLIE

NORTH SEA

WOOD ANT

BALTIC SEA

BRITISH ISLES

The many lakes in the northern European forests provide animals with places to drink.

POLECAT

KILOMETRES
0 100 200 300 400

0 100 200
MILES

ENGLISH CHANNEL

ICHNEUMON FLY

ARDENNES FOREST

NORTHERN

Wisla

Oder

EUROPE

Many European conifer forests have been planted by people and are harvested for their timber.

RED DEER

BLACK FOREST

Danube

Woodlands

THE BROADLEAVED WOODLANDS of Europe provide food and shelter for a rich variety of animals. Every tree supports its own web of life. Insects feed on the leaves, birds and mammals nest in the trunk and branches, and creatures such as woodlice and beetles live in the leaf litter on the woodland floor.

The weather changes with the seasons, and this affects the behaviour and lifestyle of the animals. In the warm spring days, insects emerge, birds begin to nest, and young mammals are born. In the hot summer months there is plenty of food, and the young animals grow quickly. In autumn, most of the trees lose their leaves, and the animals feast on fruits and berries or store food for the winter. The long, cold nights and short days make winter a difficult time for the animals. Many grow thick coats and spend more time in their burrows or tree holes. Some birds fly away to spend the winter months in warmer climates.

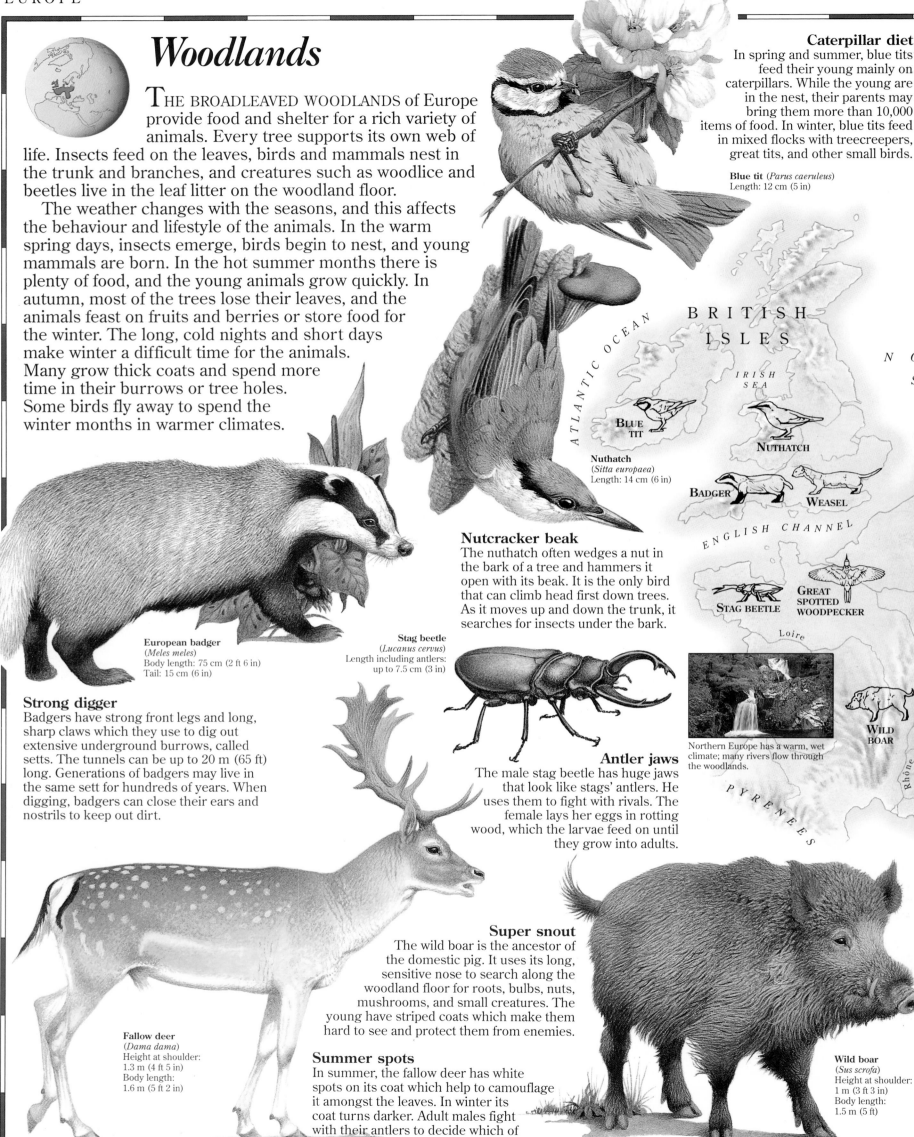

Caterpillar diet
In spring and summer, blue tits feed their young mainly on caterpillars. While the young are in the nest, their parents may bring them more than 10,000 items of food. In winter, blue tits feed in mixed flocks with treecreepers, great tits, and other small birds.

Blue tit (*Parus caeruleus*)
Length: 12 cm (5 in)

BRITISH ISLES

ATLANTIC OCEAN

IRISH SEA

BLUE TIT

Nuthatch
(*Sitta europaea*)
Length: 14 cm (6 in)

NUTHATCH

BADGER   WEASEL

ENGLISH CHANNEL

STAG BEETLE   GREAT SPOTTED WOODPECKER

Loire

WILD BOAR

Northern Europe has a warm, wet climate; many rivers flow through the woodlands.

PYRENEES

Rhône

European badger
(*Meles meles*)
Body length: 75 cm (2 ft 6 in)
Tail: 15 cm (6 in)

Strong digger
Badgers have strong front legs and long, sharp claws which they use to dig out extensive underground burrows, called setts. The tunnels can be up to 20 m (65 ft) long. Generations of badgers may live in the same sett for hundreds of years. When digging, badgers can close their ears and nostrils to keep out dirt.

Nutcracker beak
The nuthatch often wedges a nut in the bark of a tree and hammers it open with its beak. It is the only bird that can climb head first down trees. As it moves up and down the trunk, it searches for insects under the bark.

Stag beetle
(*Lucanus cervus*)
Length including antlers:
up to 7.5 cm (3 in)

Antler jaws
The male stag beetle has huge jaws that look like stags' antlers. He uses them to fight with rivals. The female lays her eggs in rotting wood, which the larvae feed on until they grow into adults.

Fallow deer
(*Dama dama*)
Height at shoulder:
1.3 m (4 ft 5 in)
Body length:
1.6 m (5 ft 2 in)

Super snout
The wild boar is the ancestor of the domestic pig. It uses its long, sensitive nose to search along the woodland floor for roots, bulbs, nuts, mushrooms, and small creatures. The young have striped coats which make them hard to see and protect them from enemies.

Summer spots
In summer, the fallow deer has white spots on its coat which help to camouflage it amongst the leaves. In winter its coat turns darker. Adult males fight with their antlers to decide which of them will mate with the females.

Wild boar
(*Sus scrofa*)
Height at shoulder:
1 m (3 ft 3 in)
Body length:
1.5 m (5 ft)

Tree acrobat

The red squirrel's long, bushy tail helps it to balance as it leaps from tree to tree. The squirrel may also use its tail to send signals to other squirrels, flicking it to warn them of danger. The squirrel has long, strong back legs and hooked claws, which help it to grip tree bark. Red squirrels usually climb down a tree head first.

Red squirrel (*Sciurus vulgaris*)
Body length: 25 cm (10 in)
Tail: 20 cm (8 in)

Prickly armour

A hedgehog has up to 5,000 spines on its back. Spines are really modified hairs. Although they are hollow, they are very strong and have sharp points. If a hedgehog is alarmed, it rolls into a ball to protect its underparts with its spines. Baby hedgehogs have soft spines so they do not scratch their mothers while suckling.

European hedgehog
(*Erinaceus europaeus*)
Length: 23 cm (9 in)

Clinging claws

The great spotted woodpecker has sharp, curved claws that help it cling tightly to tree bark. Its stiff tail feathers help to support its weight against the trunk. With its powerful, straight beak the woodpecker chisels insects out from under the bark. It uses its long, sticky tongue to reach into cracks and crevices and lick up insects.

Great spotted woodpecker
(*Dendrocopos major*)
Length: 23 cm (9 in)

Tawny owl (*Strix aluco*)
Length: 38 cm (1 ft 3 in)
Wingspan: 1 m (3 ft 3 in)

Silent wings

The tawny owl hunts at night. It has soft, fringed wing feathers which are specially suited for silent flying. It can see well in the dark and has very good hearing. Its prey are small creatures, such as mice and voles, which it seizes with its curved talons.

FALLOW DEER

RED SQUIRREL

HEDGEHOG

Elbe

RED FOX

DORMOUSE

U R O P E

TAWNY OWL

Rotting leaves litter the woodland floor and provide a rich source of food for plants and insects.

KILOMETRES
0   100   200   300
0   100   200
MILES

There are many gaps in the trees that let light down to the woodland floor.

Danube

A L P S

Common dormouse
(*Muscardinus avellanarius*)
Body length: 8 cm (3 in)
Tail: 7 cm (2.5 in)

Slim hunter

The weasel has a long, thin body which enables it to squeeze into the burrows of mice and voles and prevent them escaping. The weasel is strong for its size and can kill larger animals, such as rabbits.

Winter sleeper

The dormouse hibernates (sleeps) through the cold winter months in a warm nest of leaves and grass. Its nest may be under leaf litter or in a hollow tree stump. The dormouse eats as much as possible in the autumn and may nearly double in weight. This helps it to survive during hibernation.

Weasel (*Mustela nivalis*)
Body length: 20 cm (8 in)
Tail: 5 cm (2 in)

Red fox (*Vulpes vulpes*)
Height at shoulder: 35 cm (14 in)
Body length: 75 cm (2 ft 5 in)

Night hunter

Red foxes hunt mainly at night. They eat almost anything, from rabbits and earthworms to fish and apples. Although their natural habitat is woodland, many foxes have now adapted to live in towns. They often come out at night to search in people's rubbish bins for food.

31

Southern Europe

THE COUNTRIES OF SOUTHERN EUROPE lie around the northern coast of the Mediterranean Sea. They have a climate of long, hot, dry summers with cooler, wetter winters. The typical landscape of this region is dry scrubland.

Large numbers of people live in southern Europe or visit the area on holiday. People have destroyed most of the forests which once covered the region and polluted the sea. But there are still some refuges for wildlife, such as the Alps and Pyrenees mountains, the marshlands of the Coto Doñana in Spain, and the Camargue in France. Some rare animals, such as the chamois and the Spanish lynx, live in these protected areas. Southern Europe is also famous for its birdlife. Huge numbers of birds, such as storks, buzzards, and eagles, travel across the region on their regular migration routes between Europe and Africa.

Lammergeyer
(*Gypaetus barbatus*)
Length: up to 1.1 m (3 ft 10 in)
Wingspan: up to 2.7 m (9 ft)

Bone breaker
The lammergeyer, or bearded vulture, feeds on bones which it scavenges from dead animals. Before it starts to feed, it waits until other vultures have pecked all the meat off the bones. The lammergeyer sometimes drops bones from a great height so they crack open. It can then eat the marrow inside.

Brown bear (*Ursus arctos*)
Height at shoulder: up to 1.2 m (4 ft)
Body length: up to 3 m (9 ft 8 in)

Chamois
(*Rupicapra rupicapra*)
Height at shoulder:
up to 80 cm (2 ft 8 in)
Body length:
1 m (3 ft 3 in)

Clinging feet
The nimble, sure-footed chamois leaps about the rocky crags in mountainous areas of southern Europe. It has strong legs and a spongy pad under each hoof, which helps it to grip steep or slippery surfaces. The chamois has an incredible sense of balance. Its leaps can be more than 6 m (19 ft) long and 4 m (13 ft) high.

Blind cave-dweller
The olm, or cave salamander, lives in underground pools and streams. It has no eyes because it lives in pitch darkness and does not need to see. The olm breathes partly through the red gills on the sides of its head.

Olm
(*Proteus anguinus*)
Length: up to
30 cm (12 in)

Name call
The hoopoe is named after its call, which sounds like "hoo-poo-poo". Young hoopoes drive enemies away from their nest by producing a strong smell, hissing loudly, and poking their bills upwards.

Short-sighted bear
The brown bear is short-sighted, so it relies on its keen sense of smell to find food. This bear lives in the mountains of southern Europe. It is mostly vegetarian, and uses its long claws to dig up roots, shoots, and bulbs. In autumn, the bear fattens up on fruits and berries to last it through the winter, when it hibernates.

Hoopoe
(*Upupa epops*)
Length:
28 cm (11 in)

Green toad
(*Bufo viridis*)
Length: 10 cm (4 in)

Insect gobbler
The green toad comes out in the cool, moist night air to hunt for insects. It sometimes enters villages to hunt around street lamps and other sources of light, which attract insects. The toad has no teeth and swallows its food whole.

SOUTHER

GOLDEN ORIOLE

HOOPOE

BAY OF BISCAY

Dordogne

Garonne

ALP

GREATER FLAMINGO

Douro

CHAMOIS

BROWN BEAR

LAMMERGEYER

CORSICA

SARDINIA

SMALL SPOTTED GENET

SPANISH LYNX

BARBARY APE

BALEARIC ISLANDS

MED

ATLANTIC OCEAN

ROCK OF GIBRALTAR

MEDITERRANE MONK SEAL

The typical Mediterranean habitat consists of dry scrubland, covered with thorny shrubs and small trees.

NORTH

Small spotted genet
(*Genetta genetta*)
Body length: up to
60 cm (2 ft)
Tail: up to
48 cm (18 in)

Spotted stalker

The small spotted genet sleeps during the day and comes out at night to stalk small mammals, nesting birds, reptiles, and insects. Its keen eyesight, smell, and hearing make it an efficient hunter. The genet is a good climber. It uses its sharp claws to cling on to tree trunks and branches.

Filter beak

The greater flamingo wades through shallow water using its webbed feet to stir up shrimps and other small animals from the muddy bottom. It has special fringes inside its beak which it uses to filter these animals out of the water.

Greater flamingo
(*Phoenicopterus ruber*)
Length: 1.2 m (4 ft)
Wingspan: 1.4 m (4 ft 8 in)

Gibraltar monkey

Barbary apes live on the Rock of Gibraltar, but no-one is sure how they got there. Many centuries ago the Romans may have taken them there from North Africa. Although these creatures are called Barbary apes, they are in fact a kind of monkey.

Barbary ape
(*Macaca sylvanus*)
Body length: up to
75 cm (2 ft 6 in)

Streamer wings

The male thread lacewing butterfly has long, thin back wings which trail behind him like streamers. Large groups of males dance up and down displaying their wings. This probably helps to attract females.

Thread lacewing
(*Nemoptera sinuata*)
Wingspan:
6 cm (2 in)

Spanish lynx (*Felis lynx*)
Body length: 1.3 m (4 ft 3 in)
Tail: 8 cm (3 in)

Rare cat

The Spanish lynx was once widespread but its numbers have been drastically reduced because of hunting and the destruction of its forest habitat. Today it is only found in remote mountainous areas and in the Coto Doñana reserve. The lynx lives alone and hunts for small mammals and birds at night.

Golden oriole
(*Oriolus oriolus*)
Length: 24 cm (9.5 in)

Golden bird

The male golden oriole has bright yellow and black feathers which help him to attract a female. The female is a drab green colour. This provides camouflage when she sits on the nest. In winter, golden orioles migrate to Africa.

EUROPE

The Camargue is a marshy area in southern France, famous for its wild horses, bulls, and flamingos.

OLM

KILOMETRES
0   150   300   450

0   150   300
MILES

The Mediterranean coastline is dotted with beaches where turtles and seals come ashore to breed.

THREAD
LACEWING

GREEN
TOAD

Seal survivor

The Mediterranean monk seal is one of the rarest seals in the world. It once lived all around this sea, but the beaches where it used to rest and breed have been taken over by holidaymakers. There are probably only a few hundred monk seals left and the species faces extinction.

SICILY

CRETE

Mediterranean monk seal
(*Monachus monachus*)
Length: up to
2.7 m (8 ft 10 in)

MEDITERRANEAN   SEA

AFRICA

33

The Sahara

THE SHIFTING SANDS of the Sahara Desert stretch across 9,000,000 sq km (3,475,000 sq miles) of northern Africa, an area almost as big as the United States. The Sahara is the largest desert in the world – and it is still growing. In the baking heat of the day, the temperature soars to over 50°C (122°F) in the shade. But at night it is bitterly cold. Hardly any rain falls. In some parts of the desert there may be no rain at all for several years.

The animals that live in the Sahara have adapted to this harsh environment in a variety of ways. Many small animals hide in burrows during the day and only come out at dawn and dusk, when it is cooler. Most desert animals can go for long periods without water. Some never drink – they get all the moisture they need from the plants and insects they eat.

Furry feet
The sand cat has thick fur under its feet. The fur helps to stop it sinking into the soft sand and protects it from the heat of the sand. When it hunts, its large ears enable it to hear and locate animals from a long way off.

Sand cat (*Felis margarita*)
Height at shoulder: up to 23 cm (9 in)
Body length: up to 57 cm (22 in)

Colourful reptile
The chameleon is a reptile and can survive in higher temperatures than birds or mammals. It can change colour rapidly. It feeds on insects which it catches with its long, sticky tongue.

Chameleon
(*Chamaeleo chamaeleon*)
Length including tail:
23 cm (9 in)

Prickly hunter
The desert hedgehog spends the day in a burrow and hunts at night. Its long legs lift its body above the hot sand. One of the hedgehog's favourite meals is a scorpion, which it eats after first biting off the sting in its tail.

Desert hedgehog
(*Hemiechinus auritus*)
Length: 15 cm (6 in)

Desert scorpion
(*Androctonus australis*)
Length: 8 cm (3 in)

The Sahara contains several hot, dry, mountainous regions where few plants and animals can survive.

Sand dunes in the Sahara are called "ergs", and can be up to 180 m (590 ft) high.

MED
ATLANTIC OCEAN
ATLAS MTS
FENNEC FOX
DROMEDARY CAMEL
SOOTY FALCON
AHAGGAR MTS
BARBARY SHEEP
A F R
S A H A R A
DESERT HEDGEHOG
SPINY-TAILED AGAMA

Super sting
The desert scorpion defends itself with the sting at the end of its tail. The sting is as poisonous as the bite of a cobra and can kill a much larger animal, such as a dog, in only seven minutes.

Big ears
The fennec fox has huge ears that can be up to 15 cm (6 in) long. The large, thin surface of its ears allows heat to escape from its body, like a radiator giving off heat. This helps to keep it cool. When it hunts, the fox can hear its prey moving around.

Fennec fox (*Vulpes zerda*)
Body length: up to 41 cm (16 in)
Tail: up to 20 cm (8 in)

Champion jumper
The jerboa is like a tiny kangaroo. It can jump up to 2.5 m (8 ft) in a single bound. This helps it to escape from enemies. Its strong back legs are four times as long as its front legs. Its long tail helps the jerboa to balance when it jumps and supports its body when it is standing still.

Jerboa
(*Jaculus jaculus*)
Body length:
up to 15 cm (6 in)
Tail: 25 cm (10 in)

Flying water carrier
Sandgrouse need to drink water every day. The chicks cannot fly off to find water, so their father carries it to them. He flies to a waterhole and sits in the water until his belly feathers are soaked to the skin. When he returns, he stands while the chicks drink from his feathers.

Sandgrouse
(*Pterocles alchata*)
Length:
33 cm (13 in)

Dung beetle
(*Scarabaeus sacer*)
Length:
4 cm (2 in)

Dung roller
The dung beetle eats the dung of other desert animals. It rolls the dung into balls, then buries it in holes as food for its young. The beetle has a thick, shiny skin which reflects the Sun's rays and keeps it cool. The Ancient Egyptians believed that these beetles were sacred.

Fatty hump
The dromedary, or Arabian, camel can go without water for a few weeks. Its hump is made up mostly of fat, which provides energy when food and water are scarce. The camel has long, thick eyelashes which protect its eyes, and can close its nostrils to keep out sand.

Addax
(*Addax nasomaculatus*)
Height at shoulder:
1.2 m (4 ft)
Horns: up to 1.1 m
(3 ft 6 in)

MEDITERRANEAN SEA

Nile

RED SEA

ARABIAN PENINSULA

Lake Nasser

CHAMELEON

JERBOA

SAND CAT

SCORPION

DUNG BEETLE

ADDAX

SANDGROUSE

SAHARA DESERT

The Sahara contains many rocky plateaus, called "hammadas".

KILOMETRES
0   200   400   600   800   1000
0   200   400   600
MILES

Dromedary camel
(*Camelus dromedarius*)
Height at shoulder: 1.8 m (6 ft)
Body length: up to 3.4 m (11 ft)

Rare addax
Many addax have been killed for their skins, so they are now quite rare. The addax never drinks. It gets all the moisture it needs from the plants it eats. Its wide hooves allow it to travel quickly and easily over soft sand.

Fierce falcon
Sooty falcon chicks hatch in late summer. At this time of year many small birds migrate across the Sahara. The parent falcons catch migrating birds that stop to rest and feed them to their chicks.

Fat tail
The spiny-tailed agama is a type of lizard. If food is scarce, it can survive for up to a month on the fat stored in its tail. If an enemy attacks, the agama runs head-first into its burrow, sticks out its sharp, scaly tail and beats it from side to side.

Rock climber
Barbary sheep live in the mountains of the Sahara. They are good at climbing on the rocky crags and look more like goats than sheep. They get most of the water they need from the mountain plants they eat, so they rarely need to drink.

Sooty falcon
(*Falco araea*)
Length: 35 cm (13 in)

Barbary sheep (*Ammotragus lervia*)
Height at shoulder: up to 1 m (3 ft 3 in)
Horns: up to 76 cm (2 ft 6 in)

Spiny-tailed agama (*Uromastix acanthinurus*)
Length including tail: 25 cm (10 in)

Rainforests and Lakes

THE TROPICAL RAINFORESTS of Africa stretch in a broad band from West Africa to the edge of the Great Rift Valley. This valley is a huge trough more than 6,440 km (4,000 miles) long which was created by movements of the Earth's crust. The floor of the Great Rift Valley is studded with a series of spectacular lakes, which provide a rich habitat for wildlife.

The warm, humid environment of the rainforest is home to many animals, from okapis and forest birds to frogs, snakes, and insects. Many of the plant-eating animals feed on the leaves of shrubs that form a tangled mass beneath the giant forest trees. Leaves and fruits that fall to the forest floor decay rapidly, providing food for pigs, porcupines, and termites. Some forest animals are good at climbing, and can reach food high in the trees. Camouflage helps many animals to hide from enemies and to creep up on their prey without being seen. Unfortunately, large areas of rainforest have been destroyed for timber or to make way for farms and villages and many of the animals, such as the gorilla, face possible extinction.

Armour plating
The tree pangolin is covered in horny scales which act as a suit of armour and help to protect it from enemies. The pangolin uses its long tail as an extra hand to grasp the branches. Its grip is so strong that it can hang from branches by the tip of its tail alone. The pangolin feeds on ants and termites. It uses its strong front legs to tear open their nests, and licks up the insects with its long tongue.

Tree pangolin
(*Manis tricuspis*)
Body length: up to
45 cm (18 in)
Tail: up to 60 cm (2 ft)

Gorilla
(*Gorilla gorilla*)
Height: up to 1.8 m (6 ft)

Gentle giant
Gorillas are gentle vegetarians, and feed on leaves, stalks, bark, and fruits. They live in close-knit groups of up to 30 members, each led by an adult male. Gorillas communicate with one another using a wide range of sounds and gestures. For example, a male threatens his rivals by standing up and beating his chest. Male gorillas over 10 years old have silvery-grey hair on their backs and are nicknamed "silverbacks".

Royal antelope (*Neotragus pygmaeus*)
Body length: up to 62 cm (2 ft 1 in)
Height at shoulder: up to
30 cm (12 in)

Pencil legs
The tiny royal antelope is only the size of a rabbit and its legs are as thin as pencils. It is the smallest antelope in the world. When escaping from enemies, such as larger mammals, birds, and snakes, the royal antelope can leap as far as 2.7 m (9 ft) in one bound. The royal antelope is a shy, timid animal. It hides during the day and comes out to feed on leaves at night.

Fearsome fangs
The gaboon viper is an extremely poisonous snake, and can contain enough venom to kill 20 people. Its fangs are up to 5 cm (2 in) long, and enable it to inject poisonous venom deep into the bodies of the small animals and birds it hunts. The patterns on the viper's skin act as camouflage.

Powerful hunter
The leopard is so strong that it can drag the dead body of an animal weighing almost as much as itself. It stores large items of food in the branches of a tree to stop other animals from stealing its meals. The leopard's prey includes antelopes, monkeys, birds, fishes, and snakes. Unlike most other cats, the mother leopard does not teach her cubs how to hunt. They have to learn how to fend for themselves and are not able to survive without their mother until they are 18 months to two years old.

Okapi
(*Okapia johnstoni*)
Length: up to
2 m (6 ft 6 in)
Height at shoulder:
1.7 m (5 ft 6 in)

Gaboon viper
(*Bitis gabonica*)
Length: up to
2 m (6 ft 6 in)

Stripey legs
The stripes on the okapi's legs help to break up the outline of its body when it is standing among the trees. This hides it from enemies, such as the leopard. The okapi feeds on leaves, which it pulls from trees and bushes with its tongue. Its tongue is so long that the okapi can use it to clean its eyes and eyelids. The okapi's closest relation is the giraffe. The male okapi has short, fur-covered horns, like those of a giraffe.

Leopard
(*Panthera pardus*)
Body length: up to
1.9 m (6 ft 3 in)
Tail: up to
1.4 m (4 ft 6 in)

Wattled black hornbill
(*Ceratogymna atrata*)
Length: up to
81 cm (2 ft 8 in)

Noisy feathers
As the wattled black
hornbill flies through
the rainforest, its broad
wings make a loud
swishing noise. This is
caused by air rushing
through gaps between its
flight feathers. The strange
horny ridge along the top of
its bill is called a casque. The
bird probably recognizes the
age, sex, and species of other
hornbills from their casques.

Hippopotamus
(*Hippopotamus amphibius*)
Body length: up to
4.5 m (14 ft 9 in)
Height at shoulder:
1.5 m (5 ft)

Open wide
Hippopotamuses often
fight each other. A hippo
threatens a rival by opening
its mouth wide to show off its
long, fearsome teeth. The hippo
spends most of the day resting in
lakes and rivers, or on sand banks. It
comes out at night to munch the grass
on lake shores and river banks. A hippo
can eat up to 80 kg (180 lbs) of grass and
other plant material in one night. The
hippo has webbed toes which help it
to swim, and can stay underwater
for up to six minutes.

Chimpanzee
(*Pan troglodytes*)
Height: up to
94 cm (3 ft 1 in)

African jacana
(*Actophilornis africanus*)
Length: up to 28 cm (11 in)

Goliath frog
(*Gigantorana goliath*)
Length: up to
30 cm (12 in)

Water walker
The African jacana's
long toes help to spread
its weight and enable it to walk
over floating water plants, such as
lilies. It is sometimes called a "lily-
trotter". As it stalks over the
vegetation, it snaps up water insects
and shellfish in its pointed bill. The
African jacana sometimes hides
from enemies by sinking
under the water, leaving
only its bill and
nostrils showing.

Giant leaper
The goliath frog has long back
legs and can travel more than
3 m (10 ft) in one leap. Its
short front legs help to absorb
the impact of landing. Its giant
leaps help this huge frog to
escape from enemies. Like all
frogs, the goliath frog is a
strong swimmer. Its long back
legs and webbed feet push the
frog through the water.

Tool user
The chimpanzee is extremely intelligent and is one of the
few animals known to make and use tools. It sometimes
breaks off a twig and uses it to fish termites out of their
nest, and can also use a stone as a
hammer. The chimpanzee is
equally at home in the trees or on
the ground. It walks on all fours,
with its fingers curled up to take its
weight on its knuckles. At night,
the chimpanzee builds a nest of
twigs and branches to sleep in.

Much of the African rainforest lies
in the basin of the Zaire River.

Super snail
The giant African
snail eats all kinds of
plants. It uses its rough
tongue to scrape bits of leaf
from the plant. At the end of its
long tentacles, the snail has simple
eyes, which can tell light from dark.
It uses the shorter tentacles on its head
for smelling and feeling.

Giant African snail
(*Achatina fulica*)
Length: up to 34 cm (13 in)

KILOMETRES
0   250   500   750   1000

0   200   400   600
MILES

Lake
Chad

GULF OF
ADEN

A F R I C A

Blue Nile

White Nile

TREE
PANGOLIN

ROYAL
ANTELOPE

Niger

LEOPARD

WATTLED
BLACK
HORNBILL

AFRICAN
JACANA

OKAPI

ATLANTIC OCEAN

GOLIATH
FROG

CHIMPANZEE

GABOON
VIPER

GIANT
AFRICAN
SNAIL

GORILLA

Lake
Victoria

HIPPOPOTAMUS

GREAT RIFT VALLEY

In places the walls of the Great
Rift Valley are 1,250 m
(4,000 ft) high.

Zaire

Lake
Tanganyika

Huge flocks of flamingos live on
the lakes in the Great Rift Valley.

Lake
Nyasa

Zambezi

*INDIAN
OCEAN*

The Savannah

THE SWEEPING GRASSLANDS of the African savannah are the last place on Earth where spectacular herds of large grazing animals still survive. There are two main seasons, wet and dry. At the start of the dry season, huge herds gather together and make long journeys to find fresh grass and water. The migrating herds sometimes fill the plains as far as the eye can see.

Most of the grazing animals feed on grasses, but each species eats a different part of the grass, so they seldom compete for food. Zebras eat the tough tops of the grass stems, wildebeest eat the leafy centre, and gazelles prefer the young shoots close to the ground. The plant-eaters themselves are a source of food for the hunters of the savannah – lions, leopards, cheetahs, and wild dogs. After a kill, vultures and other scavengers move in to clean up the left-overs. In the grasses at the feet of the larger animals live lizards, snakes, and millions of insects, which all play a vital role in the life of the grasslands.

Bone cruncher
Hyaenas have massive jaws, that are strong enough to crunch through bones. They hunt in small groups at night, killing animals such as wildebeest and zebra by disembowelling them. They also eat animals killed by other hunters.

Spotted hyaena (*Crocuta crocuta*)
Height at shoulder: 91 cm (3 ft)
Body length: up to 1.6 m (5 ft 4 in)

Tireless trekker
Wildebeest trek thousands of kilometres across the savannah searching for fresh grass. Whenever they stop to rest or graze, each male stakes out a terri-tory which he guards against other males. Baby wildebeest can run soon after they are born, and in a few hours they are able to keep up with the rest of the herd.

Blue wildebeest (*Connochaetes taurinus*)
Height at shoulder: 1.4 m (4 ft 6 in)
Body length: 2.1 m (7 ft)

Super soldier
The soldier termite defends its colony from attack by enemies. It uses its head and strong jaws to stab and wound attackers.

Soldier termite (*Bellicostermes natalensis*)
Length: up to 2 cm (1 in)

Group protection
Zebras usually live in family groups, but in the dry season they gather in large herds. This helps to protect them against enemies, since many pairs of eyes and ears are more likely to spot danger. Zebra stallions sometimes kick out at enemies, such as lions, and may smash their teeth.

Burchell's zebra (*Equus burchelli*)
Height at shoulder: 1.2 m (4 ft)
Body length: up to 2.4 m (8 ft)

African elephant (*Loxodonta africana*)
Height at shoulder: up to 3.5 m (11 ft 8 in)
Trunk: up to 2.1 m (7 ft)

Giant eaters
African elephants spend up to 16 hours a day searching for enough food to support their massive bodies. A big male can weigh as much as 90 adult people. Elephants use their long trunks to reach leaves high on the trees. They are strong enough to push over trees to reach the tasty new leaves on the top branches. Each elephant uses one tusk more than the other, in the same way that people are right- or left-handed.

Cheetah (*Acinonyx jubatus*)
Body length: 2.2 m (7 ft 6 in)
Tail: 76 cm (2 ft 6 in)

Lightning cat
The cheetah relies on short bursts of incredible speed to catch its prey. It can sprint at more than 100 kph (62 mph) over short distances, but tires easily. It grips the throat of its prey with its long, pointed canine teeth. Its razor-sharp back teeth slice meat off the bones.

ATLANTIC OCEAN

White-backed vulture
(*Gyps bengalensis*)
Length: 81 cm (2 ft 7 in)
Wingspan: 2.2 m
(7 ft 3 in)

Naked neck
The naked head and neck of the white-backed vulture make it easier for the bird to poke its head inside the carcass of a dead animal when feeding. Feathers would get in the way and become dirty. Vultures soar high above the savannah and use their keen eyesight to search for dead animals.

Fast runner
In spite of its size, the black rhino is very agile and can gallop at 48 kph (30 mph) over short distances. The rhino has a hook-like upper lip, which it uses to pull bark, twigs, and leaves off bushes and trees.

KILOMETRES
0   200   400   600

0   200   400
MILES

Black rhinoceros
(*Diceros bicornis*)
Body length: 3.6 m (12 ft)
Horn: 50 cm (20 in)

...thering rainclouds indicate the ...rt of the wet season in the ...orongoro Crater, Tanzania.

Lion (*Panthera leo*)
Height at shoulder:
1 m (3 ft 3 in)
Body length: 2.5 m
(8 ft 4 in)

Sleepy hunter
The lion usually hunts at night and sleeps for about 21 hours each day. Its roars can be heard up to 8 km (5 miles) away. Lions live in family groups called "prides". A pride is made up of female relatives and their young, with one or more adult males.

Tree high
The giraffe's extra-long neck allows it to reach leaves and twigs 6 m (20 ft) above the ground – well above the heads of most other animals. The giraffe uses its long tongue and curled upper lip to strip the leaves from branches.

Giraffe
(*Giraffa camelopardalis*)
Height to head: 5.5 m (18 ft)
Neck: up to 2.4 m (8 ft)

WHITE-BACKED VULTURE

Lake Victoria

CHEETAH

ZEBRA

GREAT RIFT VALLEY

Lake Tanganyika

WILDEBEEST

ELEPHANT

WEAVER BIRD

Lake Nyasa (Lake Malawi)

BLACK RHINO

A F R I C A

GIRAFFE

THOMSON'S GAZELLE

LION

HYAENA

Zambezi

INDIAN OCEAN

A large herd of wildebeest migrate across the Tanzanian plain.

K A L A H A R I
D E S E R T

TERMITE

Acacias are one of the most common savannah trees.

Red-headed weaver
(*Anaplectes rubriceps*)
Length: 15 cm (6 in)

Jumping gazelle
Thomson's gazelles live in herds. If they sense danger, the whole herd may spring up and down with their heads and legs held stiffly and their bodies curved. This is called "pronking" or "stotting" and may confuse enemies.

Thomson's gazelle
(*Gazella thomsoni*)
Height at shoulder: 66 cm (2 ft)
Horns: up to 40 cm (16 in)

Nest weaver
The male red-headed weaver bird uses supple green twigs to weave an elaborate nest that helps to attract a female. The nest is usually fixed at the end of a twig to protect the eggs and chicks from enemies. The thick walls of the nest help to keep the chicks cool by day and warm at night.

Madagascar

MADAGASCAR is the fourth largest island in the world. It was once attached to mainland Africa, but it split off and drifted away tens of millions of years ago. This long period of isolation has allowed many unique animals to develop there. These include tenrecs, lemurs, the fossa, and two-thirds of the world's chameleons. In contrast, some common groups of animals do not occur on the island at all. There are no woodpeckers, for example, and no poisonous snakes.

One of the reasons for the wide range of wildlife on Madagascar is the varied climate and vegetation found on the island. On the east coast is an area of tropical rainforest, but the extreme south of the island is much drier, with semi-desert conditions. A backbone of mountains runs from north to south down the island, while the high central plateau is relatively cold and is covered with grassy savannah.

Ring-tailed lemur
(*Lemur catta*)
Body length: 45 cm (18 in)
Tail: 55 cm (22 in)

Smelly signals
The ring-tailed lemur marks its territory with scent produced in glands on its body. These smelly signals tell rival lemurs to keep out. The male ring-tail also uses his scent in "stink fights" with other males. He spreads scent from the glands on his wrists and arm-pits over his tail. Then he shakes his tail over his back to fan the smell towards his rival. Males may battle like this for as long as an hour. Lemurs live in troops of up to 40 members. They feed on fruit, leaves, tree bark, and grass.

Clever climber
The fossa's tail is almost as long as its body, and helps it to balance when climbing trees. The fossa's prey includes lemurs and other mammals, birds, reptiles, and insects. It often uses its front paws to catch and hold a victim, which it kills with a bite on the back of its head. The fossa is the most widespread meat-eating animal on Madagascar. It has been able to thrive there because there are no cats or dogs on the island, so it faces little competition.

Fossa
(*Cryptoprocta ferox*)
Body length: up to 75 cm (2 ft 5 in)
Tail: up to 70 cm (2 ft 3 in)

Wattled false sunbird
(*Neodrepanis coruscans*)
Length: 10 cm (4 in)

Sugar straw
The wattled false sunbird uses its long, curved beak to reach the sweet nectar hidden deep inside flowers. Its tongue curls round to form a "straw" through which it sucks up the nectar. As it feeds, the sunbird carries pollen from one flower to another and helps to pollinate the plants. In the breeding season, the male sunbird develops bare blue skin on the sides of his head. This probably helps him to attract females for mating.

Sifaka
(*Propithecus verreauxi*)
Body length: 45 cm (18 in)
Tail: 55 cm (21 in)

Strange call
The sifaka's name comes from the strange call it makes to warn other sifakas of danger – "shi-fakh! shi-fakh!". The sifaka spends much of the day resting, and sunbathes with its arms held out to catch as much warmth as possible. The sifaka's legs are much longer than its arms and help it to make amazing leaps of more than 5 m (16 ft) through the trees. Occasionally, the sifaka comes down to the ground and hops along on its back feet with its arms waving wildly over its head. It cannot run on all fours because its arms are too short.

Largest litter
The female tail-less tenrec produces the largest litter of any mammal – up to 32 young. Only about 16–20 of the young usually survive. The tail-less tenrec has a coat of stiff hairs and spines. To frighten enemies away, the tenrec raises the spines and hair on its head and back, stamps its front feet, hisses, and opens its mouth wide.

Tail-less tenrec
(*Tenrec ecaudatus*)
Body length: up to 40 cm (15 in)

Outsize ears
The aye-aye is a type of lemur. It has huge, bat-like ears and its hearing is so good that it can detect insects moving beneath the bark of trees. It uses its long, spindly middle finger to pull out juicy grubs. The aye-aye also eats plant food, such as nuts, bamboo shoots, and fruit. It lives in forests and spends most of its time in the trees. The aye-aye is now on the verge of extinction, due to the destruction of its habitat.

Aye-aye
(*Daubentonia madagascariensis*)
Head and body: 45 cm (18 in)
Tail: 55 cm (22 in)

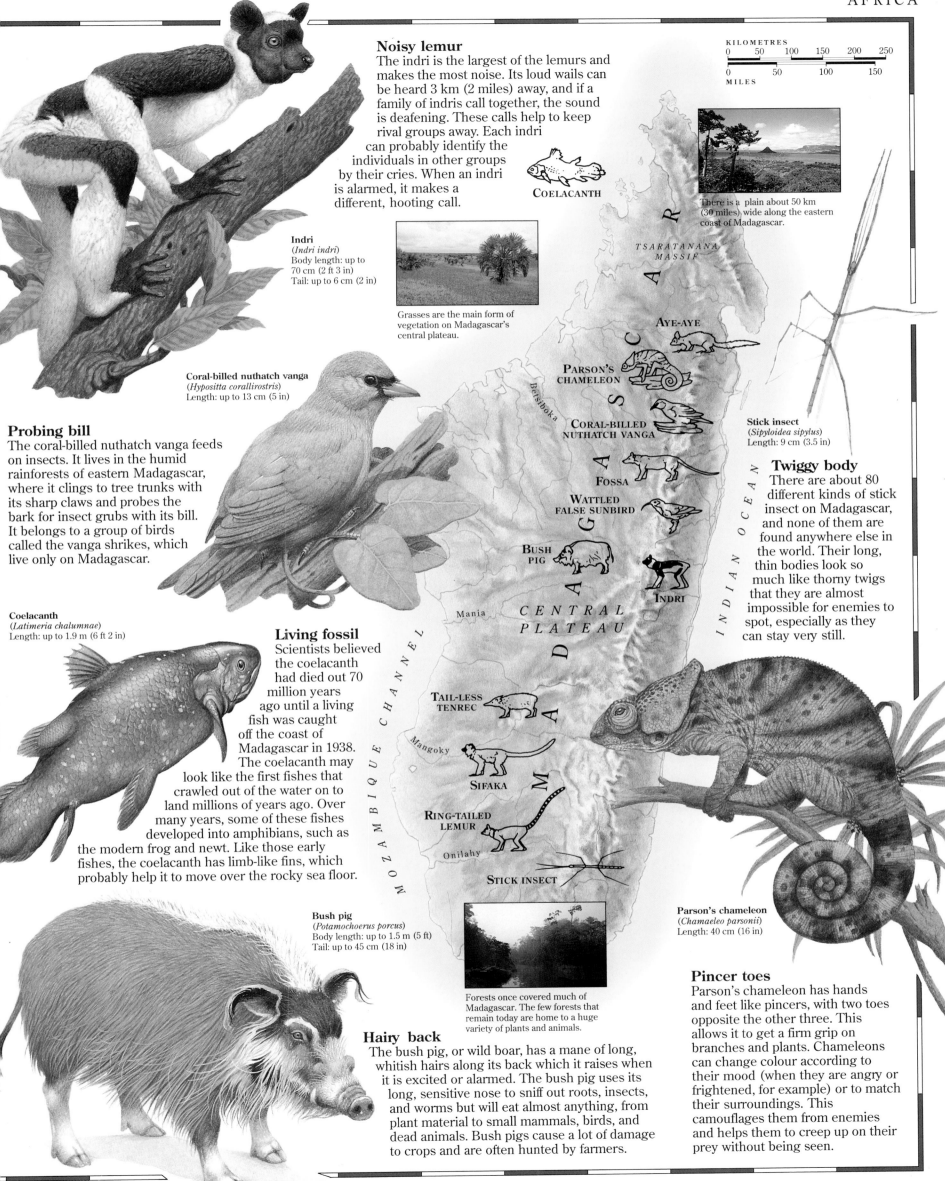

Noisy lemur

The indri is the largest of the lemurs and makes the most noise. Its loud wails can be heard 3 km (2 miles) away, and if a family of indris call together, the sound is deafening. These calls help to keep rival groups away. Each indri can probably identify the individuals in other groups by their cries. When an indri is alarmed, it makes a different, hooting call.

COELACANTH

There is a plain about 50 km (30 miles) wide along the eastern coast of Madagascar.

Indri
(*Indri indri*)
Body length: up to 70 cm (2 ft 3 in)
Tail: up to 6 cm (2 in)

Grasses are the main form of vegetation on Madagascar's central plateau.

Coral-billed nuthatch vanga
(*Hypositta corallirostris*)
Length: up to 13 cm (5 in)

Probing bill

The coral-billed nuthatch vanga feeds on insects. It lives in the humid rainforests of eastern Madagascar, where it clings to tree trunks with its sharp claws and probes the bark for insect grubs with its bill. It belongs to a group of birds called the vanga shrikes, which live only on Madagascar.

Coelacanth
(*Latimeria chalumnae*)
Length: up to 1.9 m (6 ft 2 in)

Living fossil

Scientists believed the coelacanth had died out 70 million years ago until a living fish was caught off the coast of Madagascar in 1938. The coelacanth may look like the first fishes that crawled out of the water on to land millions of years ago. Over many years, some of these fishes developed into amphibians, such as the modern frog and newt. Like those early fishes, the coelacanth has limb-like fins, which probably help it to move over the rocky sea floor.

Stick insect
(*Sipyloidea sipylus*)
Length: 9 cm (3.5 in)

Twiggy body

There are about 80 different kinds of stick insect on Madagascar, and none of them are found anywhere else in the world. Their long, thin bodies look so much like thorny twigs that they are almost impossible for enemies to spot, especially as they can stay very still.

AYE-AYE

PARSON'S CHAMELEON

CORAL-BILLED NUTHATCH VANGA

FOSSA

WATTLED FALSE SUNBIRD

BUSH PIG

INDRI

TAIL-LESS TENREC

SIFAKA

RING-TAILED LEMUR

STICK INSECT

TSARATANANA MASSIF

CENTRAL PLATEAU

MADAGASCAR

MOZAMBIQUE CHANNEL

INDIAN OCEAN

Betsiboka

Mania

Mangoky

Onilahy

Bush pig
(*Potamochoerus porcus*)
Body length: up to 1.5 m (5 ft)
Tail: up to 45 cm (18 in)

Forests once covered much of Madagascar. The few forests that remain today are home to a huge variety of plants and animals.

Hairy back

The bush pig, or wild boar, has a mane of long, whitish hairs along its back which it raises when it is excited or alarmed. The bush pig uses its long, sensitive nose to sniff out roots, insects, and worms but will eat almost anything, from plant material to small mammals, birds, and dead animals. Bush pigs cause a lot of damage to crops and are often hunted by farmers.

Parson's chameleon
(*Chamaeleo parsonii*)
Length: 40 cm (16 in)

Pincer toes

Parson's chameleon has hands and feet like pincers, with two toes opposite the other three. This allows it to get a firm grip on branches and plants. Chameleons can change colour according to their mood (when they are angry or frightened, for example) or to match their surroundings. This camouflages them from enemies and helps them to creep up on their prey without being seen.

Siberia

THE CONIFER FORESTS OF SIBERIA in northern Asia make up the largest area of forest in the world. The most common trees are larch, fir, and spruce. Their cones provide a vital source of food for animals, especially during the snowy winter months. South of the forests lies Lake Baikal. This lake has been isolated for millions of years, and many of the animals that live there are not found anywhere else in the world.

To the north of the forest belt are the barren Arctic wastes, called the tundra, where the ground is frozen for much of the year. During the winter, which lasts for nine months of the year, many animals move south to the shelter of the conifer forests and some birds fly away to warmer climates. The brief tundra summer is a time of plenty, when it is light for 24 hours a day.

Wolf
(*Canis lupus*)
Body length:
1.4 m (4 ft 5 in)
Tail: 45 cm (18 in)

Horrible howler
Wolves live in groups called packs. They howl to keep in touch with each other or to warn rival packs to keep away. A pack has a strict social order, and wolves use special body positions to signal their rank within the group. A high-ranking wolf snarls and stares at another wolf, keeping its ears and tail up in the air. A low-ranking wolf lies on its back with its ears pulled back and its tail between its legs.

Trumpet call
The whooper swan is one of the noisiest swans in the world. It gets its name from its loud, trumpeting call, which can be heard over great distances. Its wings make a swishing sound when it flies. Whooper swans often gather together in flocks of hundreds of birds. They breed in the tundra regions and on lakes deep in the conifer forests.

Whooper swan
(*Cygnus cygnus*)
Wingspan 1.5 m (5 ft)

Unique seal
The Baikal seal is the only seal that lives in fresh water. It is related to the ringed seals that live in the Arctic Ocean. Millions of years ago, its ancestors probably swam from this ocean up the River Lena to reach Lake Baikal. Now the seal cannot escape from the waters of the lake. The Baikal seal feeds on fish, snapping them up with its sharp teeth.

Baikal seal
(*Phoca sibirica*)
Length: up to 1.5 m (5 ft)

Sealing wax
The waxwing is named after the red dots on its wings. They look like drops of the wax that people used to use to seal letters. No-one knows what these markings are for. The waxwing feeds mainly on berries and digests its food very quickly. Seeds can pass through its digestive system in as little as 16 minutes.

Waxwing
(*Bombycilla garrulus*)
Length: 18 cm (7 in)

ARCTIC OCEAN

BERING SEA

EAST SIBERIAN SEA

NOVOSIBIRSKIYE OSTROVA

LAPTEV SEA

SEVERNAYA ZEMLYA

KAMCHATKA PENINSULA

KILOMETRES
0   250   500   750   1000

MILES
0   150   300   450   600

BARENTS SEA

KARA SEA

NOVAYA ZEMLYA

SIBERIAN LEMMING

Lena

Indigirka

SIBERIAN TIT

SABLE

REINDEER

SNOWY OWL

ARCTIC GROUND SQUIRREL

SIBERIAN JAY

S I B E R I A

SEA OF OKHOTSK

SAKHALIN

HAZEL GROUSE

WOLF

WAXWING

Ob

Yenisei

Angara

Lena

Lake Baikal is the deepest and oldest lake on Earth. It also contains more water than any other lake.

URAL MTS

The huge expanses of Siberian forests cover an area one-third larger than the United States.

WHOOPER SWAN

BAIKAL SEAL

Lake Baikal

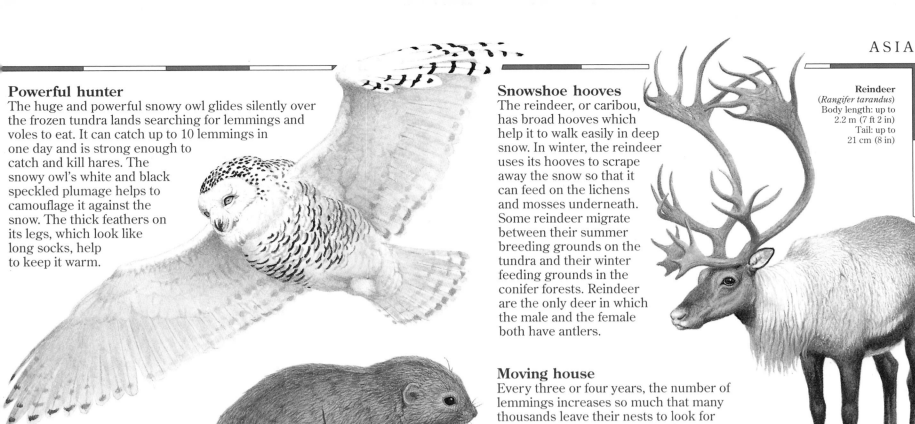

Powerful hunter

The huge and powerful snowy owl glides silently over the frozen tundra lands searching for lemmings and voles to eat. It can catch up to 10 lemmings in one day and is strong enough to catch and kill hares. The snowy owl's white and black speckled plumage helps to camouflage it against the snow. The thick feathers on its legs, which look like long socks, help to keep it warm.

Snowy owl
(*Nyctea scandiaca*)
Length: up to
66 cm (2 ft 2 in)
Wingspan: up to
1.6 m (5 ft 2 in)

Siberian lemming
(*Lemmus sibiricus*)
Length: up to
17 cm (7 in)

Snowshoe hooves

The reindeer, or caribou, has broad hooves which help it to walk easily in deep snow. In winter, the reindeer uses its hooves to scrape away the snow so that it can feed on the lichens and mosses underneath. Some reindeer migrate between their summer breeding grounds on the tundra and their winter feeding grounds in the conifer forests. Reindeer are the only deer in which the male and the female both have antlers.

Reindeer
(*Rangifer tarandus*)
Body length: up to
2.2 m (7 ft 2 in)
Tail: up to
21 cm (8 in)

Moving house

Every three or four years, the number of lemmings increases so much that many thousands leave their nests to look for new homes. Once they are on the move, lemmings will not stop, even in large towns or at busy roads. Many are eaten by enemies or die from exhaustion or starvation. Others drown trying to cross rivers, lakes, or the sea, but they do not commit suicide, as many people believe.

Underground larders

The Arctic ground squirrel stores food in its underground burrow during the short summer period. It makes several "larders" of food to last it through its winter sleep, or hibernation. It also eats a lot in the summer to build up stores of fat in its body. If the ground squirrel is frightened or senses danger, it makes a loud call to warn other ground squirrels.

Arctic ground squirrel
(*Spermophilus parryi*)
Body: up to 35 cm (14 in)
Tail: up to 15 cm (6 in)

Speckled feathers

The brown, speckled markings on the feathers of the female hazel grouse help to hide her from enemies while she is sitting on her eggs. The hazel grouse has large flight muscles, which also act as a store of food and can be used to produce heat if the grouse gets very cold. Grouse are the most common and widespread birds in the conifer forests.

Hazel grouse
(*Bonasa bonasia*)
Length: 35 cm (14 in)

Siberian tit
(*Parus cinctus*)
Length: 13 cm (5 in)

Fur coat

The sable has a beautiful, thick coat and was hunted almost to extinction for its fur. Some sables are still bred on fur farms for their skins. Others have been reared in captivity and released back into the wild, so the sable is no longer an endangered species. The sable feeds on small mammals, such as voles, as well as fish, insects, nuts, and berries. It has well-developed scent glands and uses this scent to mark the edges of its territory. These smelly messages tell other sables to keep away.

Sable (*Martes zibellina*)
Body length: up to 45 cm (18 in)
Tail: up to 19 cm (7 in)

Cone eater

The Siberian jay uses its strong beak to break open tree cones and reach the seeds inside. It sometimes holds a cone in its feet while it pulls out the seeds with its beak. The numbers of Siberian jays are closely linked to the numbers of cones on the trees – when there are few cones, their numbers fall dramatically. When food is in short supply, these jays often move into towns and villages in search of scraps.

Siberian jay
(*Perisoreus infaustus*)
Length: 28 cm (11 in)

Energy saver

The Siberian tit stays in the forests all year round, despite the freezing winter temperatures. At night, its heart-beat and other body processes slow down, and its temperature drops so that it uses up less energy. This helps it to survive when energy-giving food is hard to find. The tit uses its short, sturdy bill to pluck insects, seeds, and berries from the trees and bushes.

Deserts and Steppe

A VAST AREA OF GRASSLAND, called the steppe, stretches across the southern part of the USSR and into China. The climate in this region consists of very hot summers and long, icy winters, with cold winds blowing down from the frozen north. Huge herds of grazing animals, such as saigas and onagers, once populated the steppe, but these have been almost wiped out by hunting. Some of the remaining herds are now protected, but they are forced to live in drier areas, away from farms. Today, the most common animals on the steppe are burrowing rodents, such as the suslik.

South of the steppe lie the deserts of central Asia, where rainfall is less than 30 cm (12 in) a year. Summers are baking hot, but at night the temperature can drop by as much as 20°C (36°F). Some desert animals sleep through the summer months; others come out only at night to escape the heat of the day. Small animals, such as the jerboa, are adapted to survive without drinking. Some larger animals, such as the camel, store fat in their bodies to keep them going when food and water are scarce.

Bactrian camel
(*Camelus bactrianus*)
Height at shoulder:
up to 2 m (6 ft 6 in)
Body length: up to
3 m (9 ft 9 in)

One hump or two?
The bactrian camel has two humps, but the Arabian camel has only one. Most bactrian camels have been domesticated by people, but a small number still live wild in the Gobi Desert. This camel can survive in very high and very low temperatures. In winter it grows long, shaggy hair which keeps it warm, but in summer most of this hair falls out. It has wide, flat feet that enable it to walk over the soft sand without sinking in.

Rare eagle
The rare steppe eagle nests on the ground because there are so few trees on the open steppe grasslands. It is a fierce hunter, especially of small rodents, such as hamsters, lemmings, susliks, and marmots. The eagle swoops down out of the sky and seizes its prey with its strong, sharp talons. Then it uses its hooked beak to tear its food into bite-sized pieces.

Steppe eagle
(*Aquila nipalnesis orientalis*)
Body length: up to 86 cm (2 ft 10 in)
Wingspan: up to 1.7 m (5 ft 9 in)

Lebetine viper
(*Vipera lebetina*)
Length: 1.8 m (6 ft)

Lethal viper
The lebetine viper is one of the largest of the desert snakes. It is poisonous and kills by injecting venom into its prey through its long, hollow fangs. It waits in a concealed position to ambush and strike the rodents and lizards on which it feeds. The viper waits for its victim to die and then swallows it whole. It rests in the shade or below ground during the heat of the day, coming out at night to hunt.

Fast runner
The onager, or wild ass, can run at speeds of 65 kph (40 mph) or more – as fast as any race horse. It can go for two or three days without drinking, which helps it to survive in the dry conditions of the deserts and steppe. In summer the onager lives on the high grassland, but in winter it migrates to lower levels to find water and fresh grass to eat.

Onager
(*Equus hemionus*)
Height at shoulder:
up to 1.4 m (4 ft 7 in)
Body length: 2 m (6 ft 6 in)

Cheek pouches
The hamster feeds on seeds, grain, roots, plants, and insects. In late summer, it stores large supplies of food in a network of tunnels that it digs beneath the steppe, carrying the food to its burrow in special cheek pouches. Hamsters have been known to store as much as 10 kg (22 lb) of food. During the winter, the hamster hibernates in its burrow, waking every so often for a snack.

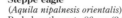

Common hamster
(*Cricetus cricetus*)
Body length: up to 30 cm (12 in)
Tail: up to 6 cm (2 in)

Monitor lizard
(*Varanus griseus*)
Length: up to 1.5 m (5 ft)

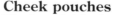

Huge lizard
The giant monitor lizard, or varan, eats almost anything, from other lizards and tortoises to rodents and birds. Sometimes it even eats its own young. It swallows its prey whole, like a snake. To frighten enemies away, the monitor lizard hisses loudly and lashes its powerful tail from side to side. It may also bite enemies. Monitor lizards are becoming rare because people kill them for their skins.

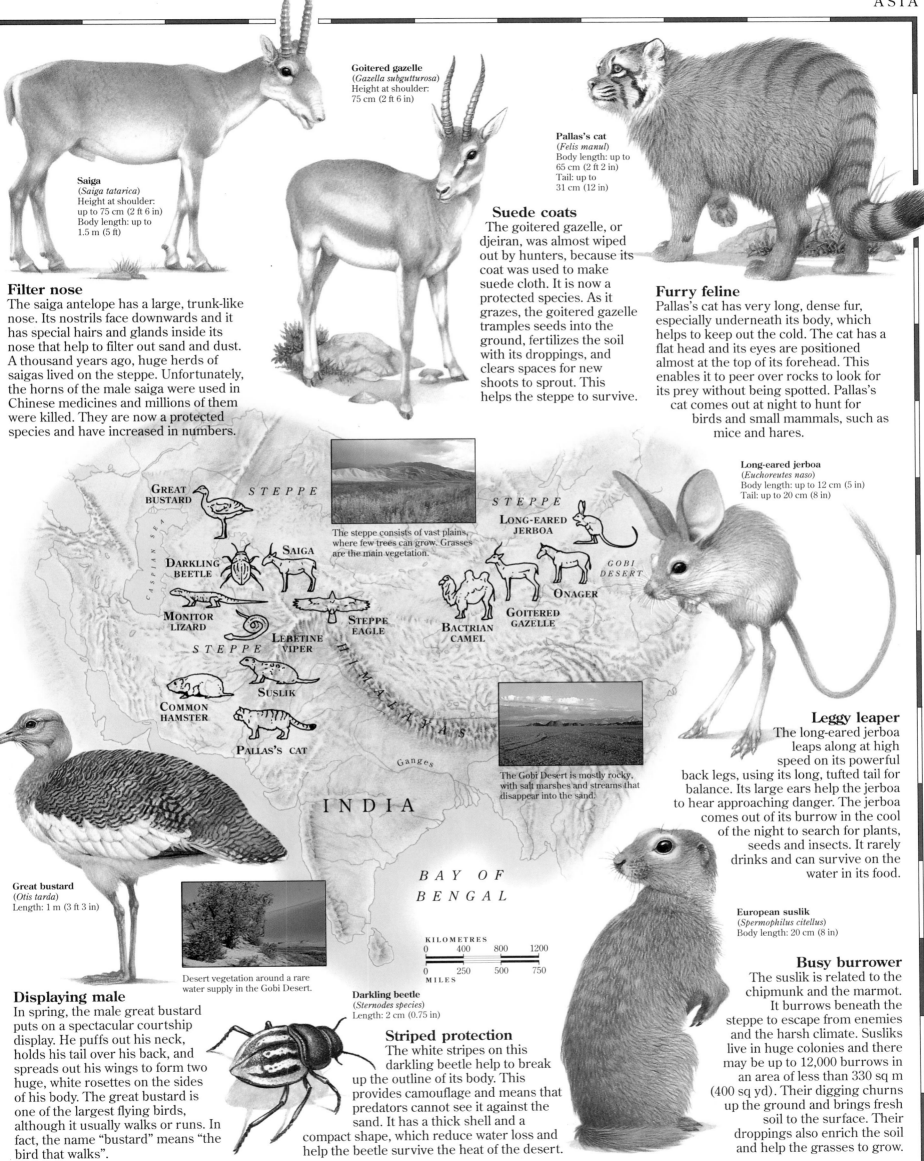

Saiga
(*Saiga tatarica*)
Height at shoulder:
up to 75 cm (2 ft 6 in)
Body length: up to
1.5 m (5 ft)

Goitered gazelle
(*Gazella subgutturosa*)
Height at shoulder:
75 cm (2 ft 6 in)

Pallas's cat
(*Felis manul*)
Body length: up to
65 cm (2 ft 2 in)
Tail: up to
31 cm (12 in)

Filter nose
The saiga antelope has a large, trunk-like nose. Its nostrils face downwards and it has special hairs and glands inside its nose that help to filter out sand and dust. A thousand years ago, huge herds of saigas lived on the steppe. Unfortunately, the horns of the male saiga were used in Chinese medicines and millions of them were killed. They are now a protected species and have increased in numbers.

Suede coats
The goitered gazelle, or djeiran, was almost wiped out by hunters, because its coat was used to make suede cloth. It is now a protected species. As it grazes, the goitered gazelle tramples seeds into the ground, fertilizes the soil with its droppings, and clears spaces for new shoots to sprout. This helps the steppe to survive.

Furry feline
Pallas's cat has very long, dense fur, especially underneath its body, which helps to keep out the cold. The cat has a flat head and its eyes are positioned almost at the top of its forehead. This enables it to peer over rocks to look for its prey without being spotted. Pallas's cat comes out at night to hunt for birds and small mammals, such as mice and hares.

Long-eared jerboa
(*Euchoreutes naso*)
Body length: up to 12 cm (5 in)
Tail: up to 20 cm (8 in)

GREAT BUSTARD — *STEPPE*

STEPPE
LONG-EARED JERBOA

The steppe consists of vast plains, where few trees can grow. Grasses are the main vegetation.

DARKLING BEETLE — SAIGA

GOBI DESERT

MONITOR LIZARD — STEPPE EAGLE — LEBETINE VIPER

BACTRIAN CAMEL — GOITERED GAZELLE — ONAGER

STEPPE

COMMON HAMSTER — SUSLIK

PALLAS'S CAT

HIMALAYAS

Ganges

The Gobi Desert is mostly rocky, with salt marshes and streams that disappear into the sand.

INDIA

Leggy leaper
The long-eared jerboa leaps along at high speed on its powerful back legs, using its long, tufted tail for balance. Its large ears help the jerboa to hear approaching danger. The jerboa comes out of its burrow in the cool of the night to search for plants, seeds and insects. It rarely drinks and can survive on the water in its food.

European suslik
(*Spermophilus citellus*)
Body length: 20 cm (8 in)

Great bustard
(*Otis tarda*)
Length: 1 m (3 ft 3 in)

BAY OF BENGAL

Displaying male
In spring, the male great bustard puts on a spectacular courtship display. He puffs out his neck, holds his tail over his back, and spreads out his wings to form two huge, white rosettes on the sides of his body. The great bustard is one of the largest flying birds, although it usually walks or runs. In fact, the name "bustard" means "the bird that walks".

Desert vegetation around a rare water supply in the Gobi Desert.

Darkling beetle
(*Sternodes species*)
Length: 2 cm (0.75 in)

KILOMETRES
0   400   800   1200

MILES
0   250   500   750

Striped protection
The white stripes on this darkling beetle help to break up the outline of its body. This provides camouflage and means that predators cannot see it against the sand. It has a thick shell and a compact shape, which reduce water loss and help the beetle survive the heat of the desert.

Busy burrower
The suslik is related to the chipmunk and the marmot. It burrows beneath the steppe to escape from enemies and the harsh climate. Susliks live in huge colonies and there may be up to 12,000 burrows in an area of less than 330 sq m (400 sq yd). Their digging churns up the ground and brings fresh soil to the surface. Their droppings also enrich the soil and help the grasses to grow.

The Himalayas

THE HIMALAYAS are a gigantic chain of mountains that stretch right across northern India – a distance of about 2,400 km (1,500 miles). The Himalayas contain many of the highest mountains in the world; snow and ice cover many of the peaks all year round. The mountain chain separates the cool Asian lands to the north from the tropical regions of northern India. There are a wide variety of different habitats in the Himalayas: tropical forests in the foothills, rhododendron and bamboo forests and grassy meadows higher up, and bleak tundra areas below the high peaks.

Only insects can survive at the high altitudes of the mountain peaks. They feed on plant spores, pollen, and other insects, which are swept up from the Indian plains by the strong winds. Most animals live further down the slopes in the forests and meadows. The mountain animals have thick fur and large lungs to help them survive the cold, wind, and thin air. Many animals, such as snow leopards and ibexes, move down to the snow-free lower slopes and valleys in winter. Others, such as marmots and bears, hibernate during the coldest months.

Graceful leaper

The Hanuman langur is a graceful monkey which can leap up to 9 m (30 ft) through the trees. Its long tail helps it to balance. The langur feeds on young leaves, fruit, and flowers and has a complex stomach and ridged teeth to help it digest its tough food. It is named after Hanuman, the Hindu monkey god, and is a sacred animal in India.

Hanuman langur
(*Presbytis entellus*)
Body length: up to 1 m (3 ft 3 in)
Tail: up to 1 m (3 ft 3 in)

Flashy colours

When it rests, the Bhutan glory folds its front wings over its back wings to hide the colourful markings. If it is disturbed by an enemy, it suddenly reveals these bright colours. This may confuse the enemy and allow the butterfly time to escape. Markings such as these are called "flash colours". The Bhutan glory flies at altitudes of 1,500–2,700 m (5,000–9,000 ft) in the Himalayan forests.

Bhutan glory (*Bhutanitis lidderdalii*)
Wingspan: up to 11 cm (4.5 in)

Blood pheasant
(*Ithaginis cruentus*)
Length: 46 cm (18 in)

High hunter

The powerful snow leopard, or ounce, feeds on wild sheep and goats, which it hunts up to 5,500 m (18,000 ft) up in the mountains. In winter, it follows its prey down into the forests. The snow leopard can make huge leaps over ravines. It has long, thick fur to help it keep warm and broad feet which stop it sinking into snow. Adult snow leopards usually live alone, roaming around their huge territories.

Snow leopard
(*Panthera uncia*)
Body length: up to 1.5 m (5 ft)
Tail: 90 cm (3 ft)

Siberian ibex
(*Capra ibex sibirica*)
Height at shoulder: 1 m (3 ft 3 in)

Red stripes

The blood pheasant is named after the red stripes on the male's feathers. These bright colours help him to attract a female for mating. The female bird has dowdy brown feathers, which help to camouflage her while she is sitting on her eggs. Blood pheasants make their nests in grass-lined gaps between large boulders. They eat pine shoots, mosses, ferns, and lichens.

Huge horns

The male Siberian ibex has huge horns which he uses in spectacular "head-butting" contests to fight rival males. The ibex can leap nimbly about on the rocky crags where it is safe from most enemies. Its thick coat helps it to survive the harsh winter months, but it also migrates to the lower slopes in winter.

Indus

Sutlej

Ganges

BOBAK MARMOT

HANUMAN LANGUR

HIMALAYAN GRIFFON VULTURE

BLOOD PHEASANT

SIBERIAN IBEX

HIMALAYAN BLACK BEAR

TAKIN

MARKHOR

WILD YAK

I N D I A

The grassy meadows on the lower mountain slopes provide food for many grazing animals.

KILOMETRES
0   100   200   300   400
0   100   200   300
MILES

Mount Everest, the highest mountain in the world, is one of the Himalayan peaks.

Corkscrew head

The markhor is a wild goat. It has huge curly horns that may grow up to 1.2 m (4 ft) long. Male and female animals both have horns, but the female's horns are smaller. The markhor's coat is short and smooth in summer but grows longer in winter to keep out the cold. It also moves down the mountains to find warmer places in winter. The markhor is nearly extinct because of hunting and diseases caught from domestic animals.

Markhor
(*Capra falconeri*)
Body length: up to 1.6 m (5 ft 2 in)
Tail: up to 14 cm (5.5 in)

Fire bird

The fire-tailed myzornis has red markings on its wings and tail, making the bird look as if it is on fire. The female's red markings are duller than those of the male. This tiny bird lives in the evergreen mountain forests of Nepal. It feeds on tree sap and nectar, which it sucks up with its bristly tongue.

Fire-tailed myzornis
(*Myzornis pyrrhoura*)
Wingspan: 13 cm (5 in)

Takin
(*Budorcas taxicolor*)
Body length: 1.2 m (4 ft)
Tail: 10 cm (4 in)

Himalayan black bear
(*Selenarctos thibetanus*)
Height at shoulder: 90 cm (3 ft)
Body length: 1.7 m (5 ft 7 in)

Winter sleep

The bobak marmot sleeps through the cold winter months in the warmth and safety of its burrow. Marmots live in groups. One animal always stands guard to warn the others of any danger. Marmots feed on plants and come out in the early morning to search for food.

Bobak marmot
(*Marmota bobak*)
Body length: 60 cm (2 ft)
Tail: up to 16 cm (6 in)

Sturdy legs

The takin has thick, strong legs and large hoofs which help it to climb the steep slopes. In summer, large herds of takin live high up on the mountains in dense rhododendron and bamboo thickets. In winter, they move down to the valleys. Their thick fur coats help to keep them warm. Young takin can follow their mother over the slopes when they are only three days old.

Furry fringe

The wild yak has a very long furry coat which reaches almost to the ground. Under the long hairs is a layer of short, dense underfur, which insulates the yak from the freezing winter temperatures. In spring, the yak moults this underfur and looks very ragged. The wild yak is nimble and sure-footed, despite its huge size. It has been hunted almost to extinction and now lives only in remote places at altitudes of about 4,500 m (15,000 ft).

Wild yak (*Bos grunniens*)
Height at shoulder: up to 2 m (6 ft 6 in)
Body length: 3 m (9 ft 9 in)

FIRE-TAILED
MYZORNIS

BHUTAN
GLORY

SNOW LEOPARD

Ganges

Snoozing bear

In winter, the Himalayan black bear sleeps in caves or tree holes because food is hard to find. It eats as much as possible in the autumn to build up fat reserves in its body. This fat keeps it alive during the winter months. The Himalayan black bear lives in the forests on the lower slopes of the mountains. It can climb well and is a good swimmer. Sometimes it curls into a ball and rolls downhill.

Himalayan griffon vulture
(*Gyps himalayensis*)
Wingspan: 1.2 m (4 ft 2 in)

Bone stripper

The harsh life in the mountains provides a plentiful supply of dead animals for the huge Himalayan griffon vulture to eat. A group of these vultures can strip a small animal, such as an antelope, to the bone in only 20 minutes. Sometimes they eat so much at one meal that they are almost too heavy to take off again.

Trees on the mountainsides soak up rain and help to hold the soil together.

BAY OF
BENGAL

The Far East

CHINA IS ONE OF THE LARGEST COUNTRIES in the world. The climate over this vast area is controlled by the wet summer monsoon winds and the bitterly cold winds that blow down from the Arctic in winter. Mountains or desert cover two-thirds of the country. These habitats provide a refuge for some of the world's rarest animals, such as the giant panda and the Siberian tiger. China also has a rich birdlife, especially pheasants and cranes. In the east of China, much of the land is intensively cultivated to provide enough food for China's population of more than a billion people.

The islands of Japan stretch for more than 1,900 km (1,200 miles) off the east coast of China. Japan has a mild climate, with warm summers, cool winters and plentiful rainfall. Broadleaved forests cover much of the land, despite dense areas of population.

Japanese macaque (*Macaca fuscata*)
Length: up to 75 cm (2 ft 6 in)
Tail: up to 30 cm (12 in)

Hot baths

Japanese macaque monkeys live in troops of up to 40 individuals, led by an adult male. Troops that live in the cold, snowy mountains of northern Japan have learnt to keep warm in winter by taking hot baths in the volcanic mountain springs. They sit in the springs with hot water right up to their necks. Their dense fur also helps to keep them warm. Other troops of this intelligent monkey have learnt to wash their food before eating it.

Sika deer
(*Cervus nippon*)
Height at shoulder:
up to 81 cm (2 ft 8 in)

Bamboo eater

The giant panda feeds mainly on bamboo. It munches its way through about 600 bamboo stems each day and spends up to 16 hours a day just eating. It has a special knob below its first finger which helps it to grasp the stems, and its throat has a tough lining to protect it from sharp splinters of bamboo. Each giant panda lives in its own territory in the misty mountain forests of south-west China. Its thick, waterproof fur helps to keep it warm and dry. Baby pandas are pink, blind, and helpless when they are born. They take their first steps when they are about three months old, but cannot walk well until they are a year old.

Giant panda
(*Ailuropoda melanoleuca*)
Body length: up to 1.5 m (5 ft)
Tail: 13 cm (5 in)

White warning

The sika deer has a patch of white fur on its rump which it fluffs up when it is alarmed. This acts as a warning signal to other sika deer. In summer, the sika deer has a chestnut coat with white spots, which helps to camouflage it among the trees. But in winter, it grows darker fur and loses most of its spots. Sika deer are very hardy animals and have been introduced to parks and forests all over the world.

Golden pheasant
(*Chrysolophus pictus*)
Length: up to 1 m (3 ft 3 in)

Whitefin dolphin
(*Lipotes vexillifer*)
Length: up to 2.4 m (8 ft)

Common tree shrew
(*Tupaia glis*)
Head and body:
up to 23 cm (9 in)
Tail: up to 23 cm (9 in)

Courting collar

The male golden pheasant has a colourful collar of feathers which he displays to attract a female during courtship. He spreads the golden feathers forwards like a fan, so that they cover his beak. Golden pheasants live in the forests of central China. They nest on the ground, and the male bird lets the female do all the work of sitting on the eggs to keep them warm. The chicks can feed themselves as soon as they hatch and can fly when they are only about a week old.

Dinosaur days

The tree shrew probably looks like the very first mammals that developed millions of years ago in the days of the dinosaurs. It is an active animal, always on the move and sniffing everything with its long, pointed nose. Tree shrews live in pairs, building a nest on the ground or among tree roots. The male marks his territory with a strong scent made by glands in his throat.

Echo-sounder

The whitefin, or Chinese river dolphin is one of the few dolphins that lives in fresh water. It has poor eyesight and finds its food by sending out high-pitched sounds and waiting for the echo to bounce back. The time this takes helps the dolphin to work out the shape of objects and how near they are. The whitefin dolphin has about 130 sharp, pointed teeth, which it uses for spearing fish. It also probes in the mud with its long snout to look for shrimps.

Red panda (*Ailurus fulgens*)
Body length: up to 64 cm (2 ft 1 in)
Tail: up to 48 cm (19 in)

Climbing panda

The red panda comes out at night, using its sharp claws to climb quickly through the trees. It feeds mainly on bamboo shoots, roots, grasses, and fruit. It often washes itself like a cat, licking a foot and then wiping the wet foot over its fur. Young red pandas can look after themselves when they are a few months old, but stay with their mother for over a year.

SIBERIAN TIGER

JAPANESE MACAQUE

SIKA DEER

SEA OF JAPAN

KOREAN PENINSULA

JAPAN

KILOMETRES
0 150 300 450 600
0 100 200 300 400
MILES

PACIFIC OCEAN

The Huang He, or Yellow River, flows right across China. It contains a lot of silt, which gives the water a yellowish colour.

JAPANESE GIANT SALAMANDER

Huang He

GIANT PANDA

RED PANDA

MUSK DEER

GOLDEN PHEASANT

CHINA

Chang Jiang

Lake Dongting

Lake Poyang

CHINESE ALLIGATOR

EAST CHINA SEA

WHITEFIN DOLPHIN

Japanese giant salamander (*Andrias japonicus*)
Length: up to 1.5 m (5 ft)

Giant from the past

The huge Japanese giant salamander is the world's largest amphibian. Salamanders like this lived on Earth about 300 million years ago, but most of today's amphibians are much smaller. The giant salamander lives in cold streams, using a flap of skin along the sides of its body to take in oxygen from the water. It also comes to the surface to take air into its lungs.

COMMON TREE SHREW

Xi Jiang

SOUTH CHINA SEA

Mountainous forest covers about 70 per cent of Japan's land area.

TAIWAN

The bamboo forests of Sichuan province in south-west China are home to the rare giant panda.

HAINAN

Siberian tiger (*Panthera tigris*)
Body length: up to 2.4 m (8 ft)
Tail: up to 90 cm (3 ft)

Largest cat

The Siberian tiger is the largest and rarest of all the big cats. It is larger, furrier, and paler in colour than tigers that live in India and Indonesia. There are probably only a few hundred Siberian tigers left in the wild. Tigers live on their own, marking the edge of their territories with scent, droppings, and scrape marks. They also roar to tell other tigers to keep away. A tiger's roars can be heard up to 3 km (2 miles) away. Tigers come out at night to hunt for wild pigs, deer, and other forest animals.

Perfumed stomach

The male musk deer has a special gland under its stomach which produces a smelly substance called musk in the breeding season. Many musk deer have been killed to obtain this gland, which is used to make the musk smell used for perfume. The male deer has canine teeth about 7 cm (3 in) long, which stick out of the sides of his mouth. In the breeding season, males fight each other with these teeth and wrestle with their necks.

Rare reptile

The timid Chinese alligator is threatened with extinction because of the destruction of its marshland habitat and collection for breeding in captivity. Today there are probably only a few hundred of these alligators left, and they are found only in the lower part of the Chang Jiang river in eastern China. The Chinese alligator sleeps or hibernates in caves or burrows during the cold, dry winter months. It comes out in spring to mate and raise a family. This alligator feeds on snails, clams, rats, and insects.

Musk deer (*Moschus moschiferus*)
Body: 1 m (3 ft 3 in)
Tail: up to 5 cm (2 in)

Chinese alligator (*Alligator sinensis*)
Length: up to 2 m (6 ft 6 in)

Southeastern Asia and India

THE CLIMATE IN INDIA is dominated by the seasonal changes caused by the monsoon winds. They bring torrential rain and violent storms in summer. Dry, cooler weather occurs in winter. There are many types of habitat in India, ranging from mangrove swamps along the coasts, to open plains, scrubland, and broadleaved forests inland. India is a meeting place for animals from the Far East and the West. As a result, many Indian animals, such as the elephant and rhinoceros, are similar to animals found in southeastern Asia or Africa.

The climate of southeastern Asia is generally warm and humid all year round, and tropical rainforests flourish. Many animals live high up in the canopy of the forest where there is more light, water, and food. Several animals, such as the colugo, glide between the trees on "wings" of skin. These rainforests are also home to one of our closest living relatives – the orang-utan – and to a huge number of insects, many of which reach a spectacular size. Much of the original rainforest has now been cleared to make way for farmland and houses, so many animals are in danger of extinction. Some of the rarest animals, such as the Javan rhinoceros, survive only in remote parts of the Indonesian islands.

Malayan tapir
(*Tapirus indicus*)
Height at shoulder: 1 m (3 ft 3 in)
Head and body: 2 m (6 ft 6 in)

Handy nose
The Malayan tapir has a long nose that it uses to pull tender shoots, buds, and fruits from the forest plants. The tapir is very timid and comes out mainly at night, when it moves quickly through the dense forest undergrowth on well-worn tracks. It is a good swimmer and may plunge into the water to escape from enemies.

Indian elephant
(*Elephas maximus*)
Body length: up to
3.6 m (12 ft)
Height at shoulder:
up to 3.2 m (10 ft 6 in)

Atlas moth
(*Attacus atlas*)
Wingspan: up to
30 cm (12 in)

King cobra
(*Ophiophagus hannah*)
Length: up to 5.5 m (18 ft)

Hooded poisoner
The king cobra has huge poison glands. A bite from this snake can kill an elephant in four hours and a person in just 15–20 minutes. King cobras are normally secretive and quiet animals, but they can be aggressive when defending their eggs. To frighten off an enemy, the king cobra hisses, raises the front of its body, and spreads out the skin around its neck to form a hood.

Wings with eyes
The eyespots on the wings of the giant atlas moth may help to divert the attention of an enemy away from the rest of its body. Birds, for instance, often peck at the "eyes" on its wings instead of the moth's real eyes. The male atlas moth has large, feathery antennae which pick up the scent given off by females that are ready to mate. This helps him to find a female among the forest trees.

Spot the difference
The Indian or Asian elephant is similar to its African relative, but has smaller ears, a more humped back, and four nails on each back foot instead of three. Only some of the males have tusks and these are usually shorter than the tusks of African elephants. Indian elephants live in herds made up of closely related individuals, led by an elderly female. The herd rests during the hottest part of the day and spends the rest of the time feeding on plant material.

Indian rhinoceros (*Rhinoceros unicornis*)
Body length: up to 4 m (13 ft)
Height at shoulder: up to 1.8 m (6 ft)

Armour plating
The Indian rhinoceros looks as if it is wearing a suit of armour because it has thick, knobbly skin with deep folds at the joints. Its skin protects it from spiky forest plants. The rhinoceros usually lives on its own and likes to be near water as it often takes baths. The Indian rhinoceros has been hunted almost to extinction for its horn, which is used in Chinese medicine.

KILOMETRES
0   200   400   600   800   1000
0   150   300   450   600
MILES

INDIAN
ELEPHANT

BLUE
PEACOCK

Indus

Ganges

INDI
RHINOC

Narmada

INDIA

Godavari

Krishna

ARABIAN SEA

KING
COBRA

B
E
B

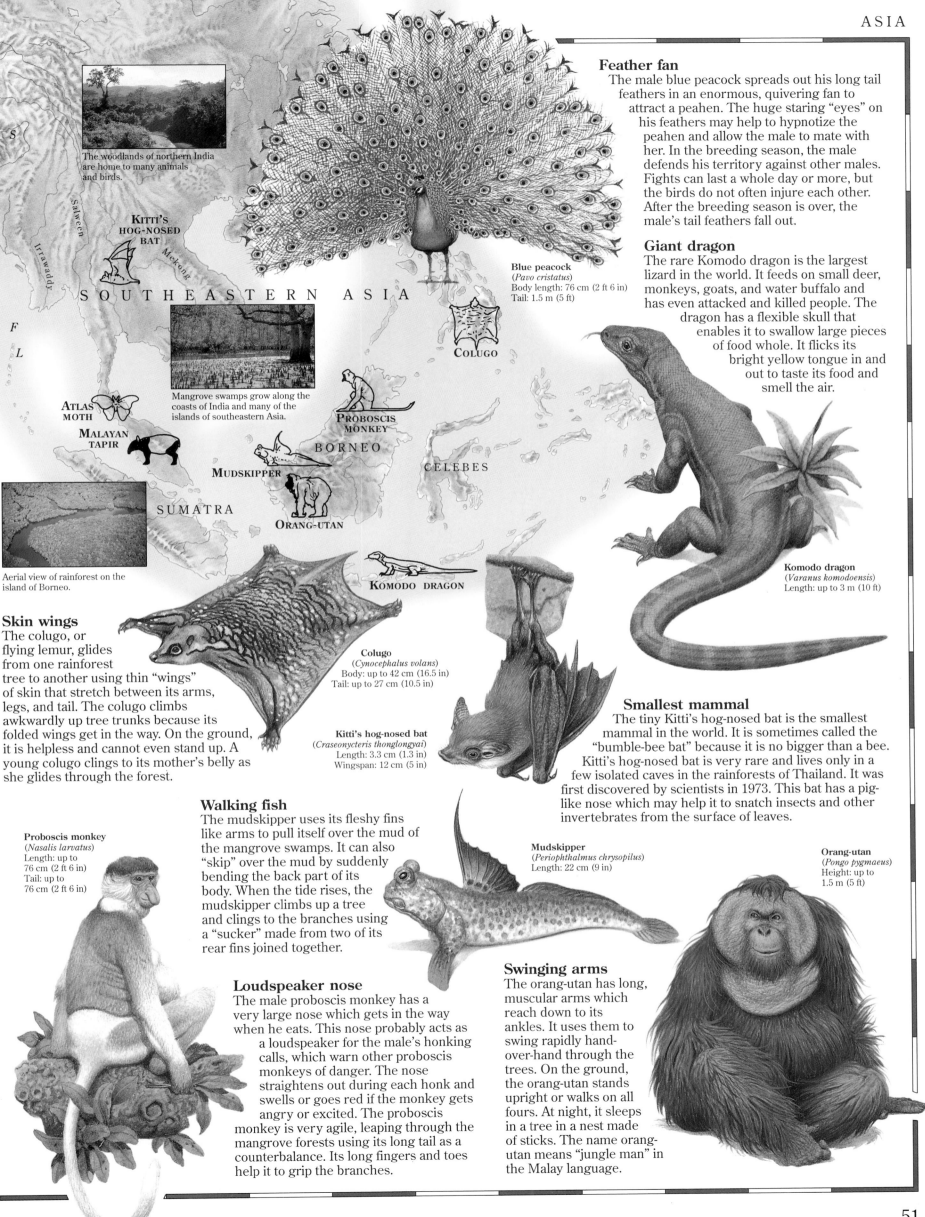

The woodlands of northern India are home to many animals and birds.

Mangrove swamps grow along the coasts of India and many of the islands of southeastern Asia.

Aerial view of rainforest on the island of Borneo.

SOUTHEASTERN ASIA

KITTI'S HOG-NOSED BAT

ATLAS MOTH

MALAYAN TAPIR

SUMATRA

BORNEO

CELEBES

PROBOSCIS MONKEY

MUDSKIPPER

ORANG-UTAN

COLUGO

KOMODO DRAGON

Feather fan

The male blue peacock spreads out his long tail feathers in an enormous, quivering fan to attract a peahen. The huge staring "eyes" on his feathers may help to hypnotize the peahen and allow the male to mate with her. In the breeding season, the male defends his territory against other males. Fights can last a whole day or more, but the birds do not often injure each other. After the breeding season is over, the male's tail feathers fall out.

Blue peacock
(*Pavo cristatus*)
Body length: 76 cm (2 ft 6 in)
Tail: 1.5 m (5 ft)

Giant dragon

The rare Komodo dragon is the largest lizard in the world. It feeds on small deer, monkeys, goats, and water buffalo and has even attacked and killed people. The dragon has a flexible skull that enables it to swallow large pieces of food whole. It flicks its bright yellow tongue in and out to taste its food and smell the air.

Komodo dragon
(*Varanus komodoensis*)
Length: up to 3 m (10 ft)

Skin wings

The colugo, or flying lemur, glides from one rainforest tree to another using thin "wings" of skin that stretch between its arms, legs, and tail. The colugo climbs awkwardly up tree trunks because its folded wings get in the way. On the ground, it is helpless and cannot even stand up. A young colugo clings to its mother's belly as she glides through the forest.

Colugo
(*Cynocephalus volans*)
Body: up to 42 cm (16.5 in)
Tail: up to 27 cm (10.5 in)

Kitti's hog-nosed bat
(*Craseonycteris thonglongyai*)
Length: 3.3 cm (1.3 in)
Wingspan: 12 cm (5 in)

Smallest mammal

The tiny Kitti's hog-nosed bat is the smallest mammal in the world. It is sometimes called the "bumble-bee bat" because it is no bigger than a bee. Kitti's hog-nosed bat is very rare and lives only in a few isolated caves in the rainforests of Thailand. It was first discovered by scientists in 1973. This bat has a pig-like nose which may help it to snatch insects and other invertebrates from the surface of leaves.

Walking fish

The mudskipper uses its fleshy fins like arms to pull itself over the mud of the mangrove swamps. It can also "skip" over the mud by suddenly bending the back part of its body. When the tide rises, the mudskipper climbs up a tree and clings to the branches using a "sucker" made from two of its rear fins joined together.

Proboscis monkey
(*Nasalis larvatus*)
Length: up to 76 cm (2 ft 6 in)
Tail: up to 76 cm (2 ft 6 in)

Mudskipper
(*Periophthalmus chrysopilus*)
Length: 22 cm (9 in)

Orang-utan
(*Pongo pygmaeus*)
Height: up to 1.5 m (5 ft)

Loudspeaker nose

The male proboscis monkey has a very large nose which gets in the way when he eats. This nose probably acts as a loudspeaker for the male's honking calls, which warn other proboscis monkeys of danger. The nose straightens out during each honk and swells or goes red if the monkey gets angry or excited. The proboscis monkey is very agile, leaping through the mangrove forests using its long tail as a counterbalance. Its long fingers and toes help it to grip the branches.

Swinging arms

The orang-utan has long, muscular arms which reach down to its ankles. It uses them to swing rapidly hand-over-hand through the trees. On the ground, the orang-utan stands upright or walks on all fours. At night, it sleeps in a tree in a nest made of sticks. The name orang-utan means "jungle man" in the Malay language.

The Outback

THE DRY, DESERT-LIKE PLAINS of the Australian outback cover more than two-thirds of the continent. Much of the region receives less than 250 mm (10 in) of rainfall a year. Although the rains may come at any time of the year, there are often long periods of drought, which make it difficult for animals to survive.

Many of the animals avoid the heat of the day by staying in their burrows, since it is cooler and damper underground. Some small animals sleep underground right through the hottest summer months. This is called aestivation. Many outback animals can survive with little or no water. Their bodies are adapted to store water from their food and to lose very little water in their urine. A number of animals have long back legs to help them move rapidly and find what little food is available.

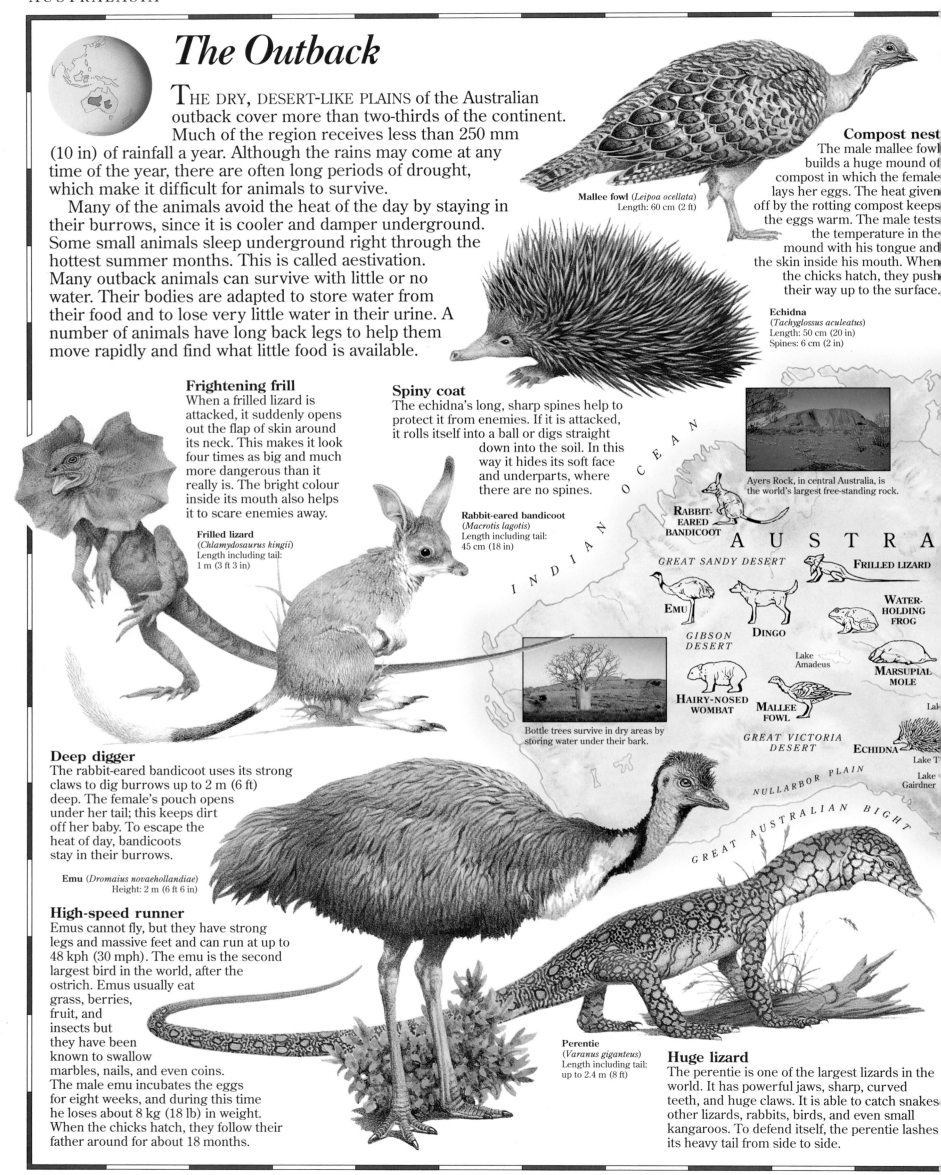

Mallee fowl (*Leipoa ocellata*)
Length: 60 cm (2 ft)

Compost nest
The male mallee fowl builds a huge mound of compost in which the female lays her eggs. The heat given off by the rotting compost keeps the eggs warm. The male tests the temperature in the mound with his tongue and the skin inside his mouth. When the chicks hatch, they push their way up to the surface.

Echidna
(*Tachyglossus aculeatus*)
Length: 50 cm (20 in)
Spines: 6 cm (2 in)

Frightening frill
When a frilled lizard is attacked, it suddenly opens out the flap of skin around its neck. This makes it look four times as big and much more dangerous than it really is. The bright colour inside its mouth also helps it to scare enemies away.

Frilled lizard
(*Chlamydosaurus kingii*)
Length including tail:
1 m (3 ft 3 in)

Spiny coat
The echidna's long, sharp spines help to protect it from enemies. If it is attacked, it rolls itself into a ball or digs straight down into the soil. In this way it hides its soft face and underparts, where there are no spines.

Rabbit-eared bandicoot
(*Macrotis lagotis*)
Length including tail:
45 cm (18 in)

Ayers Rock, in central Australia, is the world's largest free-standing rock.

INDIAN OCEAN

RABBIT-EARED BANDICOOT

A U S T R A

GREAT SANDY DESERT

EMU

DINGO

FRILLED LIZARD

WATER-HOLDING FROG

GIBSON DESERT

Lake Amadeus

MARSUPIAL MOLE

HAIRY-NOSED WOMBAT

MALLEE FOWL

GREAT VICTORIA DESERT

ECHIDNA

Lak

Lake T

Lake Gairdner

NULLARBOR PLAIN

GREAT AUSTRALIAN BIGHT

Bottle trees survive in dry areas by storing water under their bark.

Deep digger
The rabbit-eared bandicoot uses its strong claws to dig burrows up to 2 m (6 ft) deep. The female's pouch opens under her tail; this keeps dirt off her baby. To escape the heat of day, bandicoots stay in their burrows.

Emu (*Dromaius novaehollandiae*)
Height: 2 m (6 ft 6 in)

High-speed runner
Emus cannot fly, but they have strong legs and massive feet and can run at up to 48 kph (30 mph). The emu is the second largest bird in the world, after the ostrich. Emus usually eat grass, berries, fruit, and insects but they have been known to swallow marbles, nails, and even coins. The male emu incubates the eggs for eight weeks, and during this time he loses about 8 kg (18 lb) in weight. When the chicks hatch, they follow their father around for about 18 months.

Perentie
(*Varanus giganteus*)
Length including tail:
up to 2.4 m (8 ft)

Huge lizard
The perentie is one of the largest lizards in the world. It has powerful jaws, sharp, curved teeth, and huge claws. It is able to catch snakes, other lizards, rabbits, birds, and even small kangaroos. To defend itself, the perentie lashes its heavy tail from side to side.

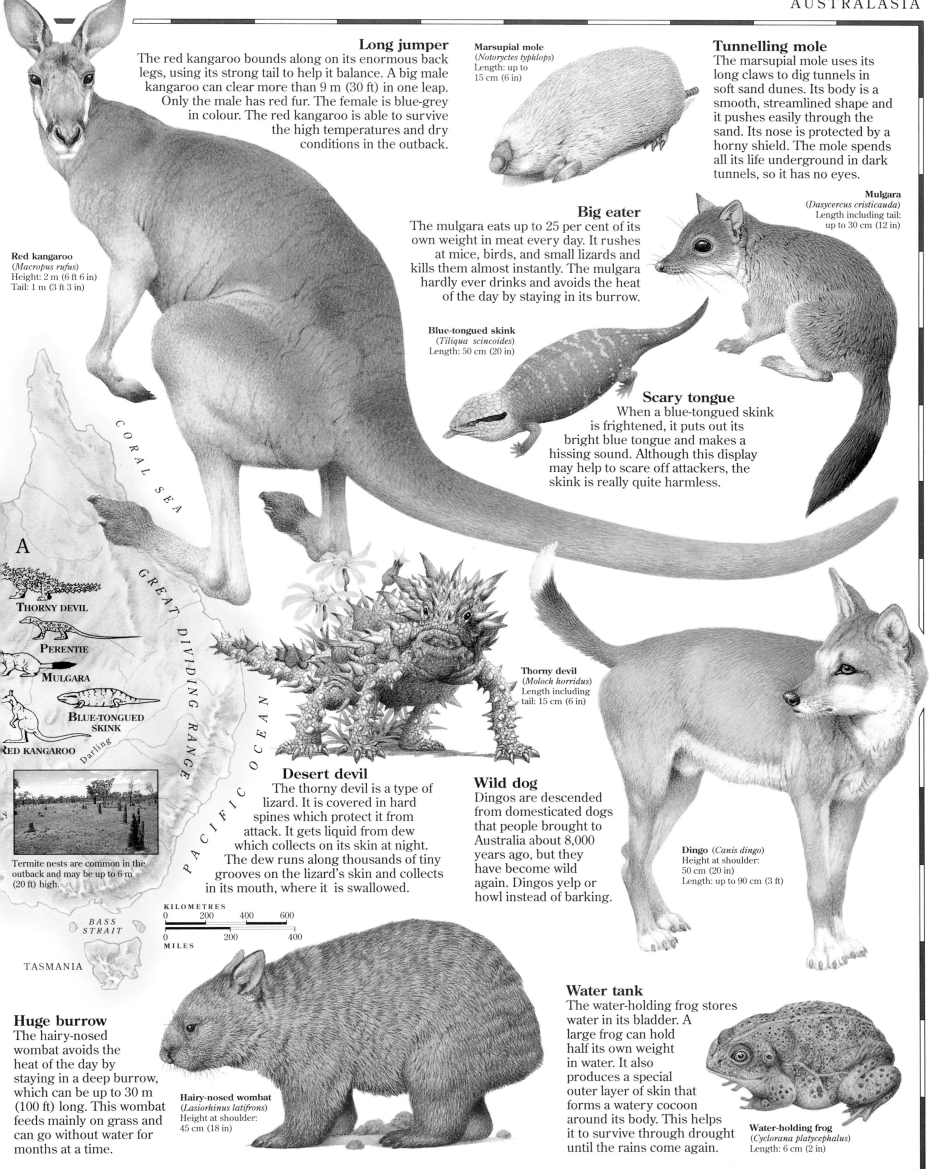

Long jumper

The red kangaroo bounds along on its enormous back legs, using its strong tail to help it balance. A big male kangaroo can clear more than 9 m (30 ft) in one leap. Only the male has red fur. The female is blue-grey in colour. The red kangaroo is able to survive the high temperatures and dry conditions in the outback.

Red kangaroo
(*Macropus rufus*)
Height: 2 m (6 ft 6 in)
Tail: 1 m (3 ft 3 in)

Marsupial mole
(*Notoryctes typhlops*)
Length: up to
15 cm (6 in)

Tunnelling mole

The marsupial mole uses its long claws to dig tunnels in soft sand dunes. Its body is a smooth, streamlined shape and it pushes easily through the sand. Its nose is protected by a horny shield. The mole spends all its life underground in dark tunnels, so it has no eyes.

Big eater

The mulgara eats up to 25 per cent of its own weight in meat every day. It rushes at mice, birds, and small lizards and kills them almost instantly. The mulgara hardly ever drinks and avoids the heat of the day by staying in its burrow.

Mulgara
(*Dasycercus cristicauda*)
Length including tail:
up to 30 cm (12 in)

Blue-tongued skink
(*Tiliqua scincoides*)
Length: 50 cm (20 in)

Scary tongue

When a blue-tongued skink is frightened, it puts out its bright blue tongue and makes a hissing sound. Although this display may help to scare off attackers, the skink is really quite harmless.

CORAL SEA

GREAT DIVIDING RANGE

PACIFIC OCEAN

A

THORNY DEVIL

PERENTIE

MULGARA

BLUE-TONGUED
SKINK

RED KANGAROO

Darling

Termite nests are common in the outback and may be up to 6 m (20 ft) high.

Desert devil

The thorny devil is a type of lizard. It is covered in hard spines which protect it from attack. It gets liquid from dew which collects on its skin at night. The dew runs along thousands of tiny grooves on the lizard's skin and collects in its mouth, where it is swallowed.

Thorny devil
(*Moloch horridus*)
Length including
tail: 15 cm (6 in)

Wild dog

Dingos are descended from domesticated dogs that people brought to Australia about 8,000 years ago, but they have become wild again. Dingos yelp or howl instead of barking.

Dingo (*Canis dingo*)
Height at shoulder:
50 cm (20 in)
Length: up to 90 cm (3 ft)

KILOMETRES
0   200   400   600

0   200   400
MILES

*BASS
STRAIT*

TASMANIA

Huge burrow

The hairy-nosed wombat avoids the heat of the day by staying in a deep burrow, which can be up to 30 m (100 ft) long. This wombat feeds mainly on grass and can go without water for months at a time.

Hairy-nosed wombat
(*Lasiorhinus latifrons*)
Height at shoulder:
45 cm (18 in)

Water tank

The water-holding frog stores water in its bladder. A large frog can hold half its own weight in water. It also produces a special outer layer of skin that forms a watery cocoon around its body. This helps it to survive through drought until the rains come again.

Water-holding frog
(*Cyclorana platycephalus*)
Length: 6 cm (2 in)

Rainforests and Woods

THE LUXURIANT TROPICAL RAINFORESTS of northeastern Australia are very different from the dry interior of the continent. They are hot and damp, providing a home for an unusual variety of animals, from tree kangaroos to spectacular birds of paradise. Similar wildlife is found in the misty mountain forests of New Guinea, an island about 2,200 km (1,500 miles) long, which lies off northeastern Australia.

In the southwest and southeast of Australia there are cooler, drier eucalyptus woods, where rain falls mainly during the winter months. Many birds nest there in the winter and early spring. The eucalyptus trees and other flowering trees and shrubs are a rich source of nectar and pollen for animals such as parrots and bats. In return, the animals help to pollinate the plants, so that seeds can develop.

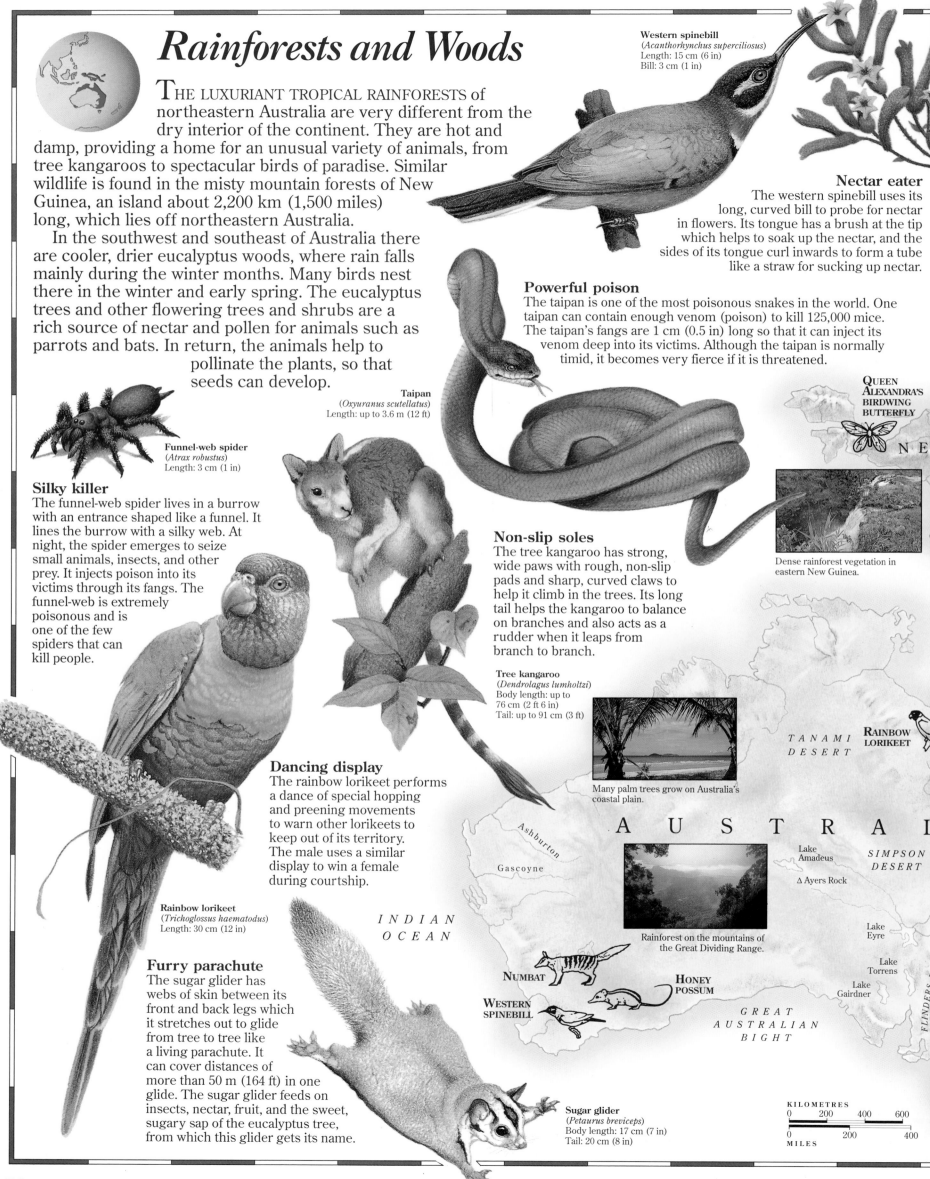

Western spinebill
(*Acanthorhynchus superciliosus*)
Length: 15 cm (6 in)
Bill: 3 cm (1 in)

Nectar eater
The western spinebill uses its long, curved bill to probe for nectar in flowers. Its tongue has a brush at the tip which helps to soak up the nectar, and the sides of its tongue curl inwards to form a tube like a straw for sucking up nectar.

Powerful poison
The taipan is one of the most poisonous snakes in the world. One taipan can contain enough venom (poison) to kill 125,000 mice. The taipan's fangs are 1 cm (0.5 in) long so that it can inject its venom deep into its victims. Although the taipan is normally timid, it becomes very fierce if it is threatened.

QUEEN ALEXANDRA'S BIRDWING BUTTERFLY

N E

Taipan
(*Oxyuranus scutellatus*)
Length: up to 3.6 m (12 ft)

Dense rainforest vegetation in eastern New Guinea.

Funnel-web spider
(*Atrax robustus*)
Length: 3 cm (1 in)

Silky killer
The funnel-web spider lives in a burrow with an entrance shaped like a funnel. It lines the burrow with a silky web. At night, the spider emerges to seize small animals, insects, and other prey. It injects poison into its victims through its fangs. The funnel-web is extremely poisonous and is one of the few spiders that can kill people.

Non-slip soles
The tree kangaroo has strong, wide paws with rough, non-slip pads and sharp, curved claws to help it climb in the trees. Its long tail helps the kangaroo to balance on branches and also acts as a rudder when it leaps from branch to branch.

Tree kangaroo
(*Dendrolagus lumholtzi*)
Body length: up to 76 cm (2 ft 6 in)
Tail: up to 91 cm (3 ft)

Dancing display
The rainbow lorikeet performs a dance of special hopping and preening movements to warn other lorikeets to keep out of its territory. The male uses a similar display to win a female during courtship.

Rainbow lorikeet
(*Trichoglossus haematodus*)
Length: 30 cm (12 in)

Furry parachute
The sugar glider has webs of skin between its front and back legs which it stretches out to glide from tree to tree like a living parachute. It can cover distances of more than 50 m (164 ft) in one glide. The sugar glider feeds on insects, nectar, fruit, and the sweet, sugary sap of the eucalyptus tree, from which this glider gets its name.

Many palm trees grow on Australia's coastal plain.

RAINBOW LORIKEET

TANAMI DESERT

A U S T R A

Lake Amadeus

SIMPSON DESERT

Δ Ayers Rock

Ashburton

Gascoyne

Rainforest on the mountains of the Great Dividing Range.

INDIAN OCEAN

Lake Eyre

Lake Torrens

Lake Gairdner

NUMBAT

HONEY POSSUM

WESTERN SPINEBILL

GREAT AUSTRALIAN BIGHT

FLINDERS

Sugar glider
(*Petaurus breviceps*)
Body length: 17 cm (7 in)
Tail: 20 cm (8 in)

KILOMETRES
0   200   400   600

0   200   400
MILES

Leafy diet

The koala has a very specialized diet – it eats only the leaves of certain types of eucalyptus trees. It has cheek pouches in which it stores the leaves and an extra long intestine to help digest them. The koala gets most of its moisture from its food and rarely drinks water. Its name comes from an Aboriginal word meaning "no drink". The koala is good at climbing trees. It can curl its fingers and toes around branches to get a good grip and has claws like knives.

Koala
(*Phascolarctos cinereus*)
Length: 80 cm (2 ft 8 in)

Queen Alexandra's birdwing butterfly
(*Ornithoptera alexandrae*)
Wingspan: up to 28 cm (11 in)

Biggest butterfly

The Queen Alexandra's birdwing butterfly is the world's largest butterfly. It is now very rare, due to over-collecting and the destruction of the rainforests. This butterfly usually flies high above the ground, where the sun filters through the trees.

Leaf-tailed gecko
(*Phyllurus cornutus*)
Length: 30 cm (12 in)

Invisible animal

During the daytime, the leaf-tailed gecko is perfectly camouflaged against the mossy tree-trunks in the rainforests. Its flattened shape means it casts few shadows, and the outline of its body is broken up by the spines along its skin.

Fantastic feathers

The male Raggiana's bird of paradise shows off his spectacular feathers to compete against other males and win a female. His performance may include hanging upside down from a branch. The female bird is quite plain in appearance.

Raggiana's bird of paradise
(*Paradisaea raggiana*)
Body length: up to 95 cm (3 ft 1 in)
Tail feathers: 50 cm (20 in)

Flower feeder

The honey possum uses its long snout to probe into flowers for pollen, nectar, and insects. It has a long, thin tongue tipped with bristles for soaking up its food.

Honey possum (*Tarsipes spenserae*)
Body length: 8 cm (3 in)

Toothy mammal

The numbat has a long tongue which it uses to lick up termites and ants. It has about 50 teeth – more than any other land mammal.

Numbat
(*Myrmecobius fasciatus*)
Body length: up to 30 cm (12 in)
Tail: up to 20 cm (8 in)

Laughing kookaburra
(*Dacelo gigas*)
Length: 45 cm (17 in)

Alarm clock bird

The kookaburra's noisy, laughing call tells other kookaburras to keep out of its territory. Kookaburras often call at dawn and wake people up. They feed mainly on mice, insects, and small snakes.

GUINEA

RAGGIANA'S BIRD OF PARADISE

SUGAR GLIDER

TREE KANGAROO

TAIPAN

AF-TAILED GECKO

KOALA

A

PACIFIC OCEAN

GREAT DIVIDING RANGE

Darling

Murray

LAUGHING KOOKABURRA

FUNNEL-WEB SPIDER

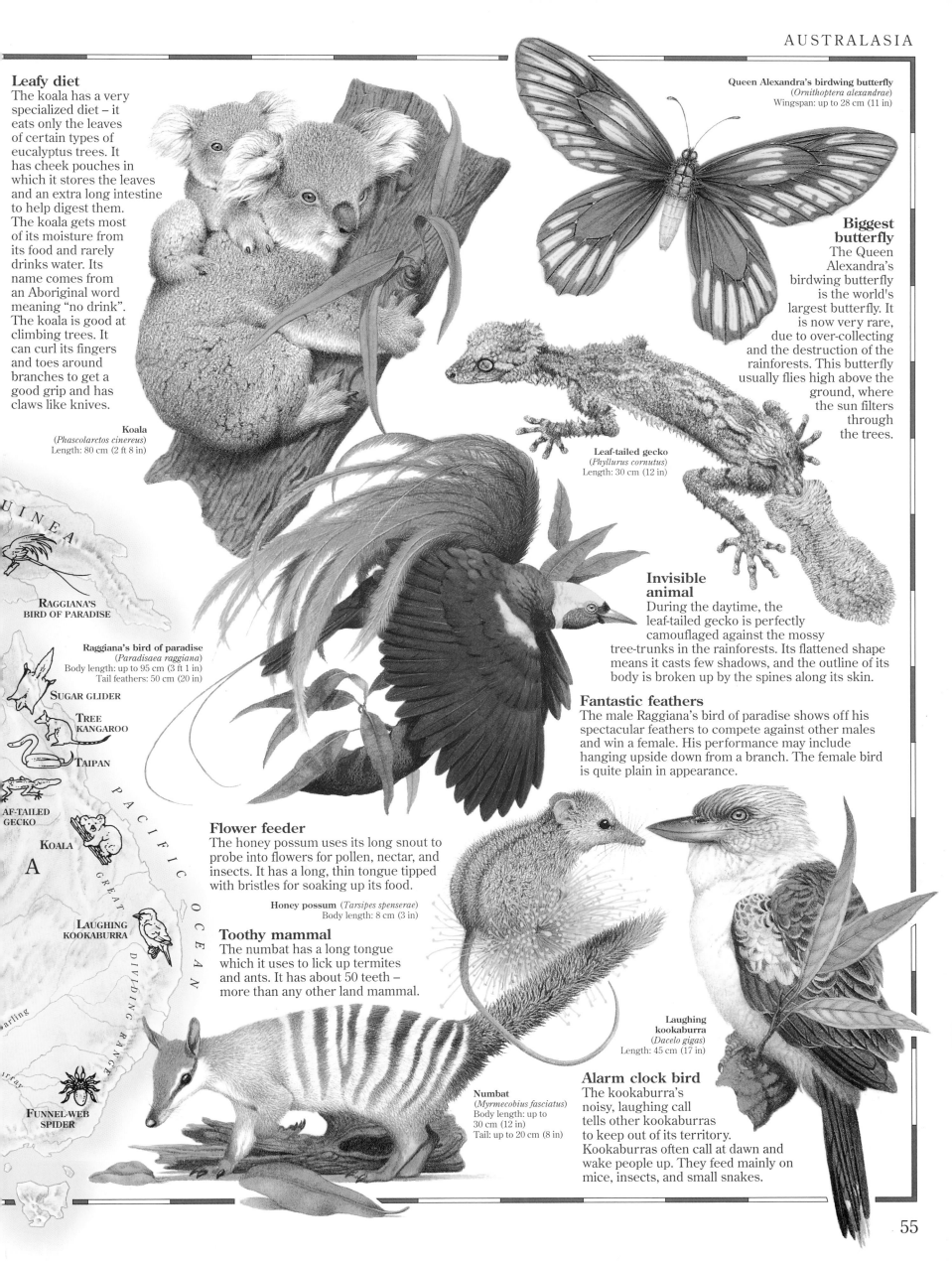

The Barrier Reef

THE BIGGEST coral reef in the world is the Great Barrier Reef, which stretches for nearly 2,000 km (1,250 miles) along the northeastern coast of Australia. Tiny animals called corals formed the reef. Over millions of years, the limestone skeletons of dead corals build up on top of one another and make a reef. This process is still going on. Reefs only form in warm, salty waters which are shallow enough for sunlight to reach the corals.

Many plants and animals can feed and grow on a reef. The Great Barrier Reef is home to a large variety of creatures, including more than 1,500 species of fish, 350 species of coral, and many types of sponge.

Stinging tentacles
This golden tubastrea coral looks like a plant, but it is really an animal. It uses stinging cells on its tentacles to catch tiny living things floating past in the water.

Golden tubastrea
(*Tubastrea aurea*)
Diameter of each
coral: 8 mm (0.35 in)

Weedy sea dragon
(*Phyllopteryx eques*)
Length: up to
25 cm (10 in)

Seaweed dragon
The weedy sea dragon is a type of fish which is covered with ragged flaps of skin. This makes it look like a piece of floating seaweed and helps to hide it from enemies. Like other seahorses, the male sea dragon carries the eggs in a special pouch on his body until they hatch.

Hinged shell
The giant clam weighs up to 250 kg (550 lbs). Its shell is in two parts, joined by a hinge. The clam usually opens its shell so that it can feed. But if danger threatens, its powerful muscles quickly heave the two halves of the shell together. Clams can live for hundreds of years.

Attractive patterns
The bright colours and patterns of butterfly fishes help them to recognize others of their own species and attract mates. To avoid competition, each kind of butterfly fish has its own place on the reef and feeds on a different kind of food.

Butterfly fish (*Chaetodon auriga*)
Length: up to 20 cm (8 in)

Crown-of-thorns starfish
(*Acanthaster planci*)
Diameter: up to
60 cm (2 ft)

Giant clam
(*Tridacna*)
Width of shell:
up to 1.5 m (5 ft)

Reef wrecker
The crown-of-thorns starfish eats coral by turning its stomach inside out and pouring digestive juices over the living coral. It leaves only the coral's skeleton behind. One starfish can eat as much as 1,800 sq cm (280 sq in) of coral in a day. These creatures have caused much damage to the Great Barrier Reef.

CAPE
YORK
PENINSULA

GREAT BARRIER REEF

WEEDY SEA
DRAGON

GIANT
CLAM

GREAT BARRIER REEF
MARINE PARK

CLEANER
FISH

CROWN OF
THORNS
STARFISH

GREAT BARRIER REEF

Cleaner fish (*Labroides dimidiatus*)
Length: up to 30 cm
(12 in)

Free food
The cleaner fish gets a free meal from other fishes on the reef. It eats their parasites (tiny animals that live on and in their bodies) and their dead scales. The cleaner fish stops larger fish from eating it by performing dances to signal that it is a friend.

Special friends
Sea anemones have poisonous tentacles that kill the small fishes they eat. The clownfish is not harmed by this poison and lives among the tentacles, where it is safe from its enemies. In return, the fish helps to lure other fish into the anemone's tentacles.

Underwater view of sea lilies, corals, and sponges.

A U S T R A L I A

CLOWNFISH
AND SEA
ANEMONE

The Barrier Reef is so big that it can be seen from the Moon.

BUTTERFLY
FISH

Clownfish
(*Amphiprion percula*)
Length: 6 cm (3 in)

When coral is not covered by sea water it loses its bright colours.

GOLDEN
TUBASTREA

KILOMETRES
0   100   200

0   50   100
MILES

GREAT BARRIER REEF
MARINE PARK

Sea anemone (*Stoichactis*)
Width: up to 1 m (3 ft 3 in)

Tasmania

THE ISLAND OF TASMANIA was once part of mainland Australia, but it is now separated from southeastern Australia by the Bass Strait. Tasmania has a cool, wet climate. The western part of the island contains large areas of rainforest which are home to many animals. Tasmania's isolation has allowed some animals to develop into unusual forms or separate species. Many rare animals live in the area around the Gordon and Franklin rivers in the southwest, which is unusual in having no cats, rats, or dogs. These mammals were brought to Australia and Tasmania by people, and have wiped out many of the native pouched mammals and birds in other areas.

Reluctant flier
The ground parrot spends most of its time on the ground. It can fly, but rarely goes more than 200 m (650 ft) before landing. The parrot is active at night, when there is less danger from enemies.

Ground parrot
(*Pezoporus wallicus*)
Length: 30 cm (12 in)

Forest demon
The Tasmanian devil's name comes from its black colouring and its eerie, whining snarl. The animal has strong jaws and teeth that can crush bones. It eats all its prey – bones, fur, skin or feathers – until nothing is left. Tasmanian devils are very shy and usually run away from people.

KING ISLAND

BASS STRAIT

Big mouth
The tiger cat is a pouched mammal which comes out mainly at night to hunt. Its jaws can open very wide and it has big, pointed teeth. The tiger cat has sharp claws and ridged pads on its back feet, which help it to climb trees.

Tiger cat
(*Dasyurops maculatus*)
Height at shoulder: 30 cm (12 in)
Body length: 70 cm (2 ft 3 in)

Bony bill
The platypus is a very unusual mammal, because it lays eggs. Its bill is made of a framework of bone covered with skin. When swimming under water, the platypus shuts its ears and eyes and uses its sensitive bill to probe for food. The platypus can stay under water for up to five minutes.

Tasmanian devil
(*Sarcophilus harrisi*)
Height at shoulder: 30 cm (12 in)
Body length: 70 cm (2 ft 3 in)

INDIAN OCEAN

Rare wolf
The thylacine or Tasmanian wolf is thought to be extinct, but a few animals may still survive in remote parts of Tasmania. The thylacine is a pouched mammal which has dog-like feet and teeth and whines, barks, and growls like a dog. But it has a thick tail like a kangaroo's. It can kill animals as large as a sheep.

PLATYPUS

Thick vegetation covers the banks of the Franklin river in southwestern Tasmania.

Lake Mackintosh

Great Lake

Many of the mountainous areas of Tasmania are covered by forest.

TASMAN SEA

T A S M A N I A

TIGER CAT

THYLACINE

RED-BELLIED PADEMELON

Lake Gordon

GROUND PARROT

TASMANIAN DEVIL

Thylacine
(*Thylacinus cynocephalus*)
Body length: 1.2 m (4 ft)
Tail: 60 cm (2 ft)

KILOMETRES
0   20   40   60
0   10   20   30
MILES

Red-bellied pademelon
(*Thylogale billardierii*)
Height: 70 cm (2 ft 3 in)
Tail: 40 cm (16 in)

Platypus
(*Ornithorhynchus anatinus*)
Length including tail:
53 cm (21 in)
Bill: 10 cm (4 in)

Tunnelling wallaby
The red-bellied pademelon is a type of kangaroo that makes tunnels through the tangled undergrowth. It lives in large groups and builds complicated networks of tunnels, rather like rabbit warrens. If a pademelon is alarmed, it may thump the ground with its back legs to warn other pademelons of approaching danger.

New Zealand

THE ISLANDS of New Zealand lie about 1,600 km (1,000 miles) east of Australia. New Zealand has a cool, wet climate in which forests and grasslands flourish.

New Zealand split off from the other landmasses about 80 million years ago, before mammals became a major group of animals. As a result, there are only two mammals native to the country, both of them bats. Birds have been able to take advantage of the lack of mammals in New Zealand, and often live in habitats that are normally used by mammals. For example, many flightless birds survive there because they can live on the ground without threat from mammal enemies.

Brown kiwi
(*Apteryx australis*)
Height: 35 cm (14 in)
Bill: 15 cm (6 in)

Crawling bat
The rare New Zealand short-tailed bat is good at moving around on the ground and can run fast on all fours, even up steep slopes. It has large, wide feet with wrinkled soles for extra grip.

Leiopelma hamiltoni
Length: up to 5 cm (2 in)

Short-tailed bat
(*Mystacina tuberculata*)
Length: up to 6 cm (2 in)

Furry feathers
The brown kiwi is a flightless bird. It is covered in long feathers which look like shaggy fur. The kiwi lives in a burrow and comes out at night to hunt for worms and insects. It finds its prey with its acute hearing and the nostrils on the tip of its sensitive bill.

Ancient frog
Frogs like the rare *Leiopelma hamiltoni* lived 150 million years ago. This frog has no eardrums or vocal sac. It develops into a froglet while it is inside the egg. The froglet has a muscular tail which it thrashes to break out of the egg.

Kea
(*Nestor notabilis*)
Length: 46 cm (18 in)

Land on the slopes of the eastern hills on the North Island is used for grazing sheep and dairy cattle.

Snow parrot
The kea is an unusual parrot which lives in the snowy Southern Alps. The kea uses its beak to dig up roots and shoots under the snow, but it also eats meat. It has been known to eat hikers' boots and to tear campers' tents to pieces.

Flightless parrot
The kakapo, or owl parrot, is the only parrot in the world that cannot fly. It has very short wings, which it uses only to glide down from trees, but it can run very fast. It comes out at night to hunt for berries, roots, leaves, and lizards.

Evergreen trees and tree ferns are the most common plants in New Zealand's forests.

Kakapo
(*Strigops habroptilus*)
Length: 63 cm (2 ft 1 in)

The Southern Alps contain many lakes, which were carved out by glaciers during the Ice Age.

Tuatara
(*Sphenodon punctatus*)
Length: up to 60 cm (2 ft)

Special survivor
The tuatara is related to a group of reptiles which lived during the age of the dinosaurs. The male can raise the spines along his back to scare off other animals. The name tuatara means "peaks on the back" in the Maori language. Tuataras can live for 120 years.

Map labels: BAY OF PLENTY, TUATARA, NORTH ISLAND, RAUKUMARA RANGE, Lake Taupo, BROWN KIWI, HAWKE BAY, TARARUA RANGE, TASMAN MTS, TASMAN BAY, COOK STRAIT, LEIOPELMA HAMILTONI, PACIFIC OCEAN, TASMAN SEA, SOUTHERN ALPS, SOUTH ISLAND, CANTERBURY PLAINS, KEA, SHORT-TAILED BAT, KAKAPO, STEWART ISLAND

KILOMETRES 0 50 100 150
MILES 0 25 50 75 100

Antarctica

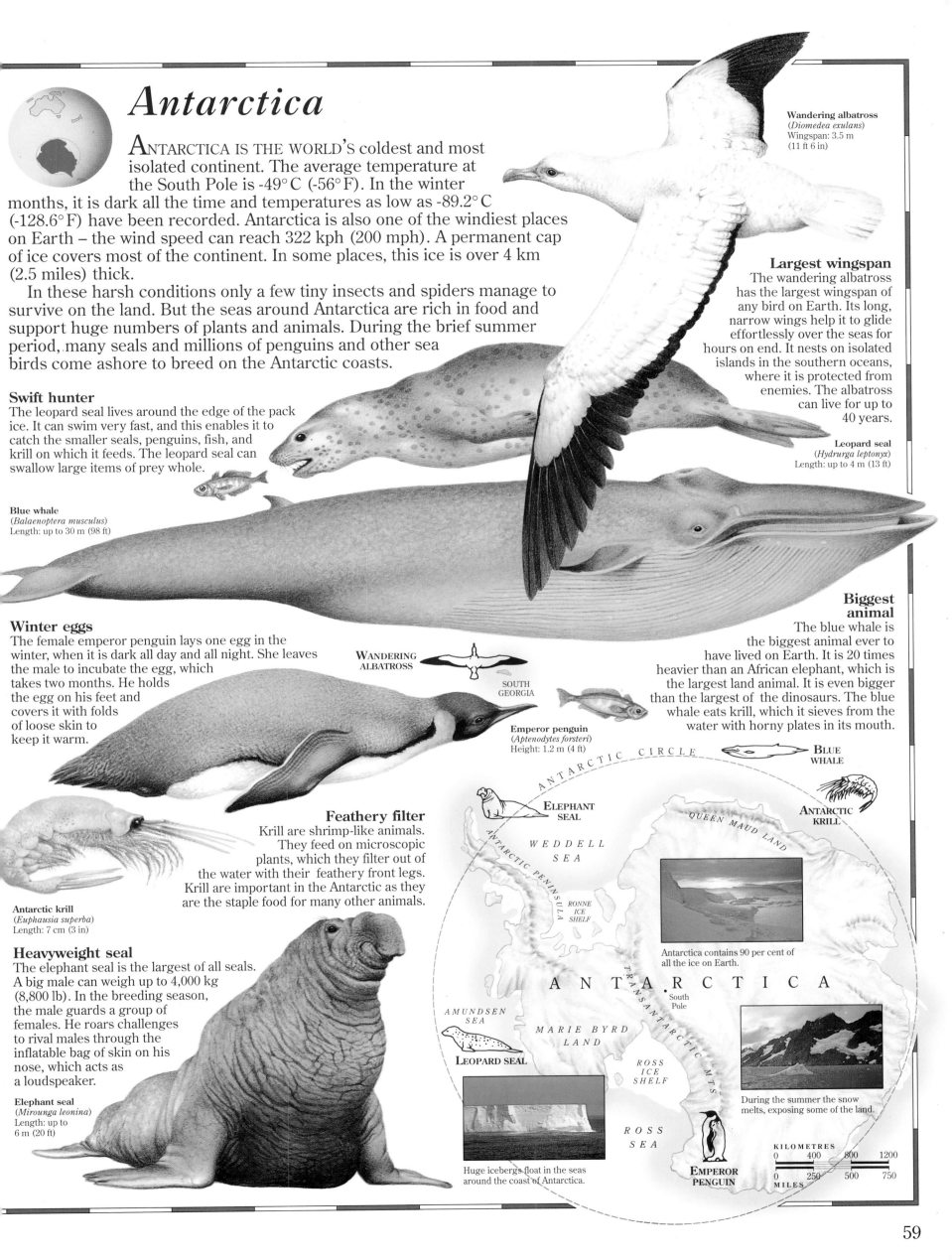

ANTARCTICA IS THE WORLD'S coldest and most
isolated continent. The average temperature at
the South Pole is -49°C (-56°F). In the winter
months, it is dark all the time and temperatures as low as -89.2°C
(-128.6°F) have been recorded. Antarctica is also one of the windiest places
on Earth – the wind speed can reach 322 kph (200 mph). A permanent cap
of ice covers most of the continent. In some places, this ice is over 4 km
(2.5 miles) thick.

In these harsh conditions only a few tiny insects and spiders manage to
survive on the land. But the seas around Antarctica are rich in food and
support huge numbers of plants and animals. During the brief summer
period, many seals and millions of penguins and other sea
birds come ashore to breed on the Antarctic coasts.

Wandering albatross
(*Diomedea exulans*)
Wingspan: 3.5 m
(11 ft 6 in)

Largest wingspan
The wandering albatross
has the largest wingspan of
any bird on Earth. Its long,
narrow wings help it to glide
effortlessly over the seas for
hours on end. It nests on isolated
islands in the southern oceans,
where it is protected from
enemies. The albatross
can live for up to
40 years.

Leopard seal
(*Hydrurga leptonyx*)
Length: up to 4 m (13 ft)

Swift hunter
The leopard seal lives around the edge of the pack
ice. It can swim very fast, and this enables it to
catch the smaller seals, penguins, fish, and
krill on which it feeds. The leopard seal can
swallow large items of prey whole.

Blue whale
(*Balaenoptera musculus*)
Length: up to 30 m (98 ft)

Biggest animal
The blue whale is
the biggest animal ever to
have lived on Earth. It is 20 times
heavier than an African elephant, which is
the largest land animal. It is even bigger
than the largest of the dinosaurs. The blue
whale eats krill, which it sieves from the
water with horny plates in its mouth.

Winter eggs
The female emperor penguin lays one egg in the
winter, when it is dark all day and all night. She leaves
the male to incubate the egg, which
takes two months. He holds
the egg on his feet and
covers it with folds
of loose skin to
keep it warm.

**WANDERING
ALBATROSS**

**SOUTH
GEORGIA**

Emperor penguin
(*Aptenodytes forsteri*)
Height: 1.2 m (4 ft)

Feathery filter
Krill are shrimp-like animals.
They feed on microscopic
plants, which they filter out of
the water with their feathery front legs.
Krill are important in the Antarctic as they
are the staple food for many other animals.

Antarctic krill
(*Euphausia superba*)
Length: 7 cm (3 in)

Heavyweight seal
The elephant seal is the largest of all seals.
A big male can weigh up to 4,000 kg
(8,800 lb). In the breeding season,
the male guards a group of
females. He roars challenges
to rival males through the
inflatable bag of skin on his
nose, which acts as
a loudspeaker.

Elephant seal
(*Mirounga leonina*)
Length: up to
6 m (20 ft)

**ANTARCTIC
CIRCLE**

**ELEPHANT
SEAL**

**BLUE
WHALE**

**ANTARCTIC
KRILL**

QUEEN MAUD LAND

**WEDDELL
SEA**

ANTARCTIC PENINSULA

**RONNE
ICE
SHELF**

Antarctica contains 90 per cent of
all the ice on Earth.

A N T A R C T I C A

**South
Pole**

**AMUNDSEN
SEA**

**MARIE BYRD
LAND**

TRANSANTARCTIC MTS

LEOPARD SEAL

**ROSS
ICE
SHELF**

**ROSS
SEA**

During the summer the snow
melts, exposing some of the land.

Huge icebergs float in the seas
around the coast of Antarctica.

**EMPEROR
PENGUIN**

KILOMETRES
0   400   800   1200

0   250   500   750
MILES

Amazing animals

Biggest animal
The blue whale is the largest sea mammal and the biggest animal that has ever lived on Earth. An adult can weigh up to 150 tonnes (147 tons). Its huge tongue alone weighs about 4 tonnes (3.9 tons).

Biggest bird
The African ostrich is the largest bird in the world. Males can be up to 2.7 m (9 ft) tall and weigh 156 kg (345 lb). Ostriches are also the fastest two-legged animals, running at speeds of up to 72 kph (45 mph).

Longest wings
The wandering albatross has the largest wingspan of any living bird. Its wings can measure over 3.5 m (11 ft 6 in) from one tip to the other. This albatross sometimes flies 900 km (560 miles) in a day.

Royal giant
The Queen Alexandra's birdwing butterfly of Papua New Guinea is the largest and heaviest butterfly in the world. It has a wingspan of up to 28 cm (11 in).

Largest on land
The African elephant is the largest land animal in the world. A large male weighs about 6 tonnes (5.9 tons) and is 3.5 m (11 ft 8 in) tall at the shoulder. One tooth from an adult elephant weighs 4.5 kg (10 lbs).

Long tail
The male quetzal of Central America has huge tail feathers that are more than twice the length of his body. He uses them to attract a mate, and sheds them after the breeding season.

Skyscraper neck
The giraffe towers up to 5.5 m (18 ft) above the African grasslands. Its long neck contains only seven vertebrae – the same as humans and all other mammals. A giraffe's tongue is 45 cm (18 in) long.

Smallest bird
The Cuban bee hummingbird is the smallest bird in the world. An adult male is only 6 cm (2 in) long; half of its length is taken up by its bill and tail.

Heaviest insect
The goliath beetle weighs up to 100 g (3.5 oz) and is the heaviest living insect.

Smallest mammal
The rare Kitti's hog-nosed bat from Thailand is the smallest land mammal. It has a wingspan of only 15 cm (6 in) and weighs no more than 2 g (0.07 oz).

Fastest flyer
The peregrine falcon is the fastest living creature, reaching speeds of at least 180 kph (112 mph) when it dives through the air in pursuit of its prey.

Fastest runner
The African cheetah can run at speeds of up to 100 kph (62 mph) over short distances, but it tires easily and has to stop to recover.

Champion jumper
A common flea can do a high jump of 19 cm (7.7 in) – 130 times its own height. It can do a long jump of 33 cm (13 in).

Huge homes
Some African termites build tall, narrow nests over 8 m (26 ft) high. One nest may contain up to 5 million termites.

Slow mover
The South American three-toed sloth moves along the ground at speeds of only 2 m (6 ft 6 in) a minute. In the trees it is a little faster, reaching a top speed of about 3 m (10 ft) a minute.

Egg-beater
The ocean sunfish lays more eggs than any other fish. One female was found to be carrying 300 million eggs.

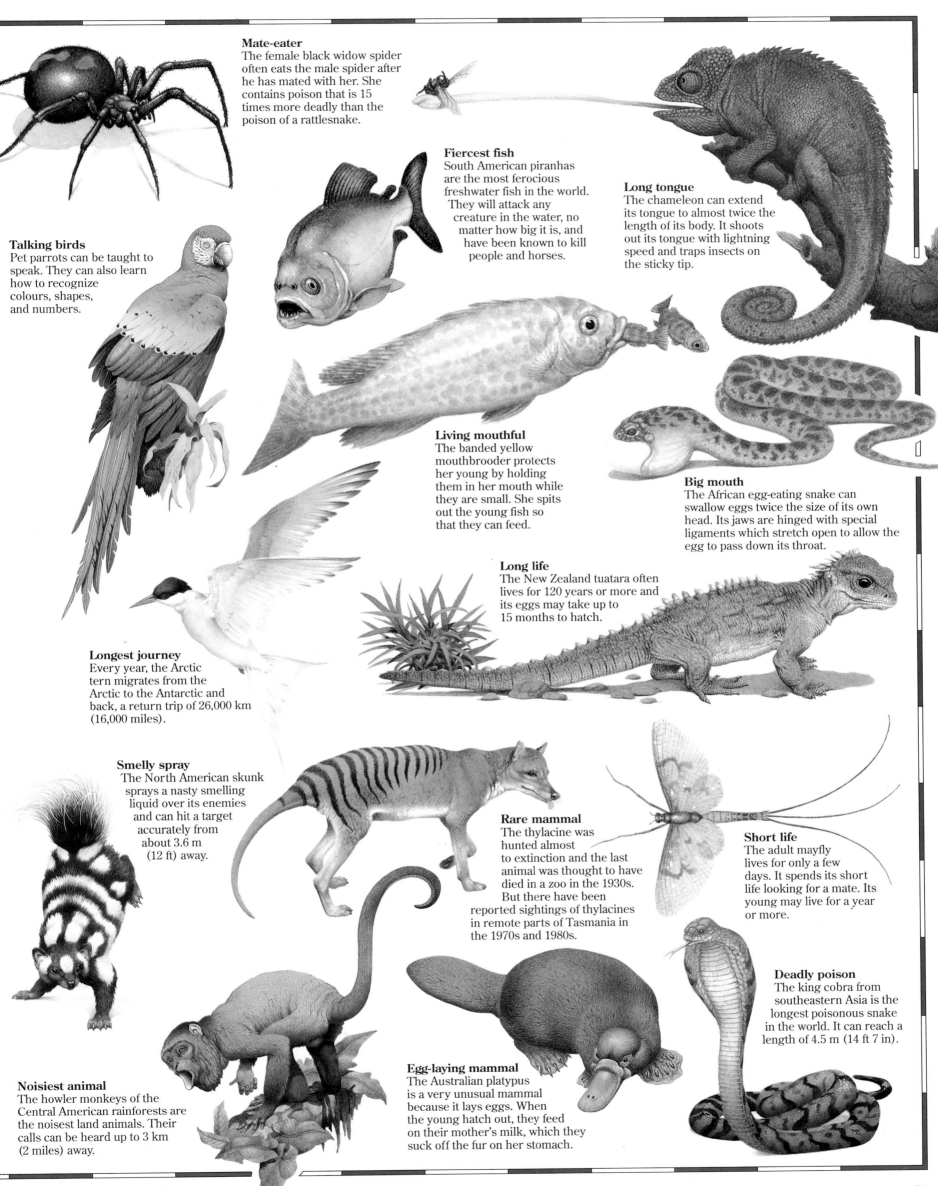

Mate-eater
The female black widow spider often eats the male spider after he has mated with her. She contains poison that is 15 times more deadly than the poison of a rattlesnake.

Fiercest fish
South American piranhas are the most ferocious freshwater fish in the world. They will attack any creature in the water, no matter how big it is, and have been known to kill people and horses.

Long tongue
The chameleon can extend its tongue to almost twice the length of its body. It shoots out its tongue with lightning speed and traps insects on the sticky tip.

Talking birds
Pet parrots can be taught to speak. They can also learn how to recognize colours, shapes, and numbers.

Living mouthful
The banded yellow mouthbrooder protects her young by holding them in her mouth while they are small. She spits out the young fish so that they can feed.

Big mouth
The African egg-eating snake can swallow eggs twice the size of its own head. Its jaws are hinged with special ligaments which stretch open to allow the egg to pass down its throat.

Long life
The New Zealand tuatara often lives for 120 years or more and its eggs may take up to 15 months to hatch.

Longest journey
Every year, the Arctic tern migrates from the Arctic to the Antarctic and back, a return trip of 26,000 km (16,000 miles).

Smelly spray
The North American skunk sprays a nasty smelling liquid over its enemies and can hit a target accurately from about 3.6 m (12 ft) away.

Rare mammal
The thylacine was hunted almost to extinction and the last animal was thought to have died in a zoo in the 1930s. But there have been reported sightings of thylacines in remote parts of Tasmania in the 1970s and 1980s.

Short life
The adult mayfly lives for only a few days. It spends its short life looking for a mate. Its young may live for a year or more.

Deadly poison
The king cobra from southeastern Asia is the longest poisonous snake in the world. It can reach a length of 4.5 m (14 ft 7 in).

Noisiest animal
The howler monkeys of the Central American rainforests are the noisiest land animals. Their calls can be heard up to 3 km (2 miles) away.

Egg-laying mammal
The Australian platypus is a very unusual mammal because it lays eggs. When the young hatch out, they feed on their mother's milk, which they suck off the fur on her stomach.

Animals in danger

IMAGINE A WORLD WITHOUT elephants, rhinos, and giant pandas. It would be tragic if these creatures vanished forever. Animals make our world a more beautiful and interesting place to live in. They are also very useful to people. We depend on some animals for food, medicines, and for helping us to grow crops and carry heavy loads.

Since life began on Earth about 3,500 million years ago, as many as 500 million species of plants and animals may have lived on our planet. Over millions of years, some of these plants and animals died out because of changes in the environment. New species developed which were better suited to the changed conditions and they replaced the older species. This slow process of change is called evolution. Some species survive for tens of millions of years without evolving much at all. Others die out after only a few thousand years.

Nowadays, species are becoming extinct much faster than they would do naturally because people hunt them or destroy their habitats. This is likely to upset the delicate balance of life on the planet. You can find out more about some of the things that threaten animals across the bottom of these two pages. Three-quarters of the extinctions that happened in the last 300 years were caused by people. At the moment, scientists believe that thousands of species of plants and animals are endangered and may become extinct by the year 2000. This includes 1,000 species of bird and over 500 mammals. Some of the most endangered species in the world are shown on this map. There are many ways in which we can help to protect endangered animals – you can read about some of them on the next page.

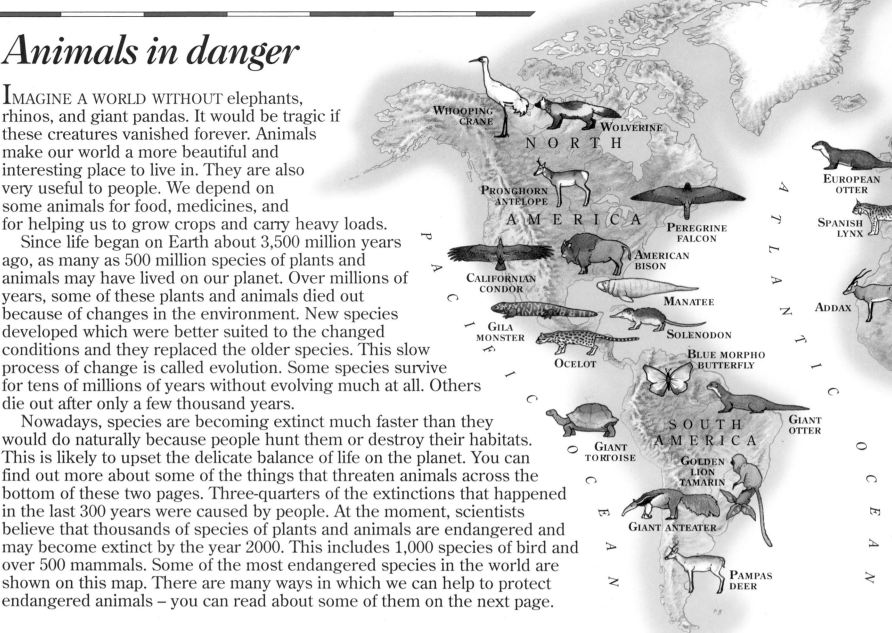

HABITAT DESTRUCTION

Spanish lynx

The main threat to the survival of endangered animals comes from people destroying their habitat. Each species of animal is suited to its particular surroundings and cannot usually move elsewhere if this habitat is destroyed. People have cut down forests for their timber or to make way for farms, mines, roads, and cities, endangering animals such as the Spanish lynx or gorilla that once lived there. Once the trees are removed, the soil may be washed away by the rain or blown away by the wind, creating land which is no use to people or animals. Marshlands and swamps are drained to provide more space for the rapidly increasing human population. Hedges are dug up to make huge fields where farm machines can work more easily. Land may also be flooded to make reservoirs that supply cities with water or to produce electricity inside large dams. In some countries, large areas of countryside have been destroyed to extract minerals or fuel from under the ground.

There are probably only about 300 mountain gorillas left in central Africa. They are threatened mainly by the destruction of their forest habitat.

Since 1945, more than half the rainforests in the world have been destroyed. Every minute, an area of rainforest the size of 80 hockey pitches is destroyed. At this rate, all the rainforests could disappear within the next 50 years.

HUNTING AND COLLECTING

Blue morpho butterfly

Many animals are hunted for sport or for valuable parts of their bodies. Animals with beautiful skins, such as leopards, cheetahs, ocelots, and caimans, are killed so that their skins can be made into coats, shoes, or bags. Most of this killing is illegal, but as long as people are willing to pay for the goods, the trade will go on. Often animals are killed for one part of their body, such as their horns or tusks, and the rest of the body is just left to rot. Rhinos, for example, are killed for their horns, which are made into dagger handles and Chinese medicines.

In the past, many animals were taken from the wild to become part of scientific collections. Nowadays, scientists are more interested in preserving wild animals in their natural habitats. But some wild animals are still collected for medical research, or to be sold as pets. Rare butterflies, such as the blue morpho, are endangered by butterfly collectors, while many rare birds are put at greater risk of extinction by people who steal their eggs for collections.

People have killed many ocelots for their spotted coats, and the species is now very rare. The rats they used to eat have increased in numbers and spread diseases.

Fur coats are a luxury. We can survive without them, and we can even make artificial fur coats which look just like the real thing. These fur coats would look much better on the animals they came from.

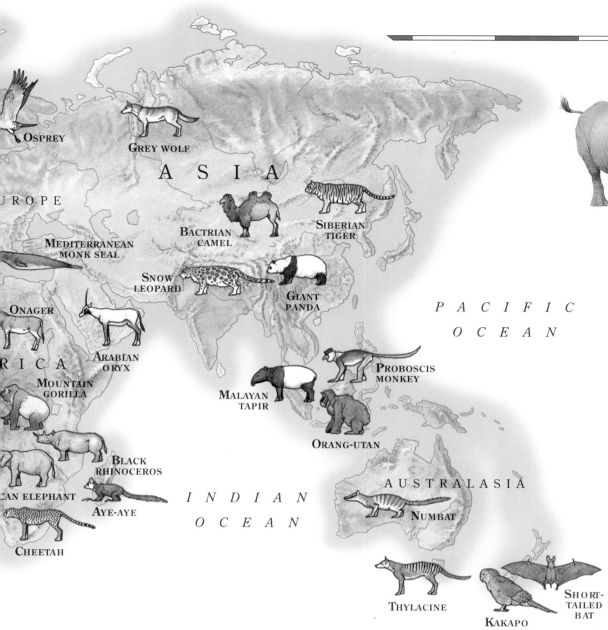

OSPREY

GREY WOLF

A S I A

BACTRIAN CAMEL

SIBERIAN TIGER

MEDITERRANEAN MONK SEAL

SNOW LEOPARD

GIANT PANDA

P A C I F I C
O C E A N

ONAGER

ARABIAN ORYX

PROBOSCIS MONKEY

MALAYAN TAPIR

MOUNTAIN GORILLA

BLACK RHINOCEROS

ORANG-UTAN

AN ELEPHANT

AYE-AYE

I N D I A N
O C E A N

A U S T R A L A S I A

NUMBAT

CHEETAH

THYLACINE

KAKAPO

SHORT-TAILED BAT

WHAT WE CAN DO TO HELP

Black rhinoceros

• Stop buying goods made from rare animals, such as fur coats, skin bags and shoes, ivory carvings, or shell jewellery.
• Set aside areas of land or water as national parks or wildlife sanctuaries, where animals can live safely with as little disturbance as possible.
• Breed endangered animals in captivity in zoos or wild animal parks. This is especially important in places where it is not possible to save the animals' habitat from being destroyed. Captive-bred animals could be released back into the wild in the future if a suitable home is found.
• Pass laws to ban the hunting of rare species.
• Reduce the amount of pollution, so that animals are not killed or harmed by poisonous materials in the environment.
• Take care of the countryside by keeping to paths, taking litter home, and being careful not to disturb wild animals.
• Stop animals, such as parrots, being taken from the wild and sold as pets.
• Stop the use of wild animals, such as chimpanzees, in medical research.
• Join conservation organizations to protest against the things that threaten the survival of rare animals, raise money for projects, and make other people more aware of the problems.
• Carry out research to find out as much as possible about the natural lives of rare animals so that we can plan the best way to protect them.

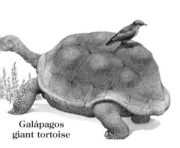

Galápagos giant tortoise

INTRODUCED SPECIES

People take animals from one country to another. Some of these introduced species are not suited to their new home and die out. Others flourish and increase in numbers, upsetting the balance of life among animals already living in the country. On the Galápagos Islands, for instance, introduced goats compete with the native giant tortoises and land iguanas for food, while introduced rats and wild cats eat baby tortoises, birds, and their eggs. Flightless birds in New Zealand, such as the kakapo, are endangered because introduced cats, rats, stoats, and ferrets eat their eggs and young.

Some species are introduced to a country to solve one problem but end up causing much more serious problems. Cane toads were introduced to Australia to eat beetles which were destroying the sugar cane crop. These poisonous toads spread fast because there were no natural enemies in Australia to control their numbers. They now threaten the survival of native frogs, reptiles, and small mammals.

Osprey

POLLUTION

Many farmers use chemicals to help them grow bigger and better crops, and to fight pests and diseases. But these chemicals seep into the soil and rivers and may poison wildlife. Poisonous chemicals from factories and sewage works may also be dumped into rivers or the sea. Another form of pollution, acid rain, is caused when the chemicals from vehicle exhausts, power stations, and factories join up with water in the air and fall as rain. Rainwater collects in streams and rivers and flows into lakes, making their waters more acidic and killing the fish that live there. Birds such as ospreys eat the fish and suffer because the poisons become concentrated in their bodies. They may lay eggs with thin shells, and have chicks with deformed bones. Acid rain also destroys forests, particularly conifer trees with needle-like leaves, reducing the habitats available for animals.

A particularly dangerous form of pollution is radioactivity. In 1986, an accident at the Chernobyl nuclear power station in the Ukraine released high levels of radiation into the air, which drifted over much of Europe. The effects of this radiation on wildlife are still being investigated.

Farmers have introduced large herds of grazing animals, such as sheep and cattle, to the grassy plains of the pampas in South America. This has changed the landscape, as farmers often start fires to encourage the growth of new grass for cattle to eat.

Large herds of pampas deer once grazed on the pampas, but competition from farm animals has drastically reduced their numbers.

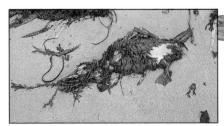

Oil sometimes escapes into the sea after a tanker runs aground or hits another ship. Oil makes birds' feathers stick together, so they cannot keep out the cold and wet or dive for food. They eventually die from cold and hunger.

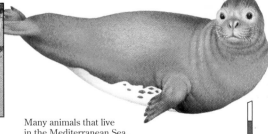

Many animals that live in the Mediterranean Sea, such as this rare Mediterranean monk seal, have been affected by pollution. The water has been polluted by oil, sewage, and industrial chemicals, making it difficult for some species to survive.

INDEX

ACKNOWLEDGMENTS

Dorling Kindersley would like to thank the following:
Rachel Foster and David Gillingwater for additional design help, Struan Reid for editorial assistance, and Lynn Bresler for compiling the index.

Picture research Cynthia Hole

Maps Aziz Khan

Picture Credits
A=above, B=below, C=centre, L=left, R=right, T=top

Bryan and Cherry Alexander Photographers: 9T; 9BL; 9BR; 59T
Heather Angel: 7C; 51C
Ardea: 49CR
J.Allan Cash Photolibrary: 5BR; 5BL; 5CR; 6TR; 6TC; 23T; 33TL; 46L; 49BL; 51T; 54T; 62L
Bruce Coleman Ltd: 16; 37BL; 41B; 47
Richard Czapnik: 34BR

Dorling Kindersley/Dave King: 5TR
Chris Fairclough Colour Library: 10T; 11; 13C; 13R; 15; 18; 30; 31TL; 31BR; 32; 34TL; 35; 39T; 39C; 39B; 52T; 52B; 53; 54C; 54B; 57TL; 58BL; 58C; 58TR; 59CR
Geoscience Features Picture Library: 5CL; 20BL; 29BR; 46R
Robert Harding Picture Library: 5TL; 7CL; 7T; 7CR; 7BL; 37T; 41T; 45T; 45BL; 51B
Hutchison Library: 13L; 15TL; 17; 27BL; 37BR; 45CR; 49T
Image Bank: 6TL; 7BR; 15B; 17B; 19T; 19B; 29T; 29CL; 33BR; 56CR; 59BL
Peter Johnson/NHPA: 41C

John Massey Stewart: 42R
Tony Morrison/South American Pictures: 6B; 23B; 23C; 27T
Papilio: 20TC; 20TR; 24; 25L; 25R
Photographers Library: 57BR
Power Pix: 56TL; 56BL
Rex Features: 62R
Travel Photo International: 10B; 27BR; 42L; 63L
Rose Winall/ICCE: 63R